EVERYTHING
WORKS

EVERYTHING
WORKS

MIKE McCARDELL

HARBOUR PUBLISHING

Harbour Publishing Co. Ltd.
P.O. Box 219, Madeira Park, BC, V0N 2H0
www.harbourpublishing.com

Cover photograph by Nick Didlick
Edited by Ian Whitelaw
Text design by Astrid Handling
Printed and bound in Canada

Harbour Publishing acknowledges financial support from the Government of Canada through the Canada Book Fund and the Canada Council for the Arts, and from the Province of British Columbia through the BC Arts Council and the Book Publishing Tax Credit.

Library and Archives Canada Cataloguing in Publication

McCardell, Mike, 1944-
    Everything works / Mike McCardell.

ISBN 978-1-55017-512-7

    1. Life change events—Humor. 2. McCardell, Mike, 1944-.
3. Television journalists—British Columbia—Vancouver—Biography.
4. British Columbia—Anecdotes. I. Title.

PN4913.M36A3 2010   C818'.602   C2010-904247-6

For everyone, yes everyone, at Global, past and present.
You helped give me the best life ever.

Contents

The End of
the Day

I was feeling sad. I don't often get that way, not since I met Reilly. You learned about him in the last book. He was the autistic kid who taught me that you get what you want if you want it badly enough and believe you'll get it. That last part is the hardest. It is also what makes it work.

I wanted a good day but the sun was setting and I was running out of time. Okay, face reality. Not every day, not every single day without let-up for more than seven years, can be good. Impossible. On this day I had found nothing new and wonderful and I felt empty.

I was coming back from the library and had just paid $14 in overdue fines. That was my fault. My wife is a pre-school teacher and she has library cards in five cities of the lower mainland and every week she borrows at least twenty books to read to the kids.

She has me review them. "You think this is good for the kids? I don't understand it."

I read it. "I don't understand it either," I say. "It sounds like it was written by a committee. They want to be so politically correct they forgot the story."

Two more are boring. One is trying to teach the kids new words, but I don't understand the vocabulary. The other has a twist at the end where the boy playing hockey turns out to be a girl who then turns out to be a mother. I read it three times and I still don't get it.

It is not easy to be in pre-school.

I read another one. "Oh, my gosh. This is great. I wish I could write like this. It has a story. It has suspense. It has a twist at the end that I understand. It has super pictures. It has comedy. Read this to them. Pleeeaase, read it." I am so excited.

In fact, to be truthful, I learned almost everything I know about writing stories for television from reading books for children. And I learned what to avoid from bad ones. I sit in parking lots reading *Tommy Went To The Circus*, and *Ruby's Big Day*.

Sometimes people ask me what books I recommend.

"There's a story with Turple the turtle," I say. "She loses one of her legs when it gets tangled in some fishing line that someone has left in the water but she still grows up to have ten wonderful children whom she plays with and she teaches them to be careful around piles of plastic string."

I show them the book. "This is what life is about; suffering, tragedy and overcoming it, joy and making the world better. There's no better story."

In fact, if it wasn't for children's books I would not know how to put anything on television. I once read a fancy, high-class text on how to do television news. It talked about framing a picture so the object is three-quarters of the way to the top and not crossing an axis so that the viewer always gets the scene in a 180-degree radius but never 181 degrees because that would be too hard on the eye and the viewer would lose concentration.

First of all, that is silly. Can you imagine anyone in front of a television concentrating?

"Yes, for a hundred dollars I think Hudson Bay is a department store."

Blaaaaaa! (The loser's horn.)

"What do you mean it's a body of water? That's not fair. I will file a discrimination suit against this show for picking on people just because they don't know things."

But not crossing the axis is important. Just as it is important to nod in a "cut away" picture of the reporter, which means a shot of the reporter taken after an interview is over. "In that way," says the instructional book, "your viewers will think you are actually listening."

After reading that, I wanted to go back to newspapers where you only had to know something, then close your eyes and type. Actually, closing your eyes was never taught in journalism school either. What they want you to do is take lots of notes, which replaces actually listening to a person, summarize everything in the first sentence and then write the story in descending order of importance until you run out of things to say, which means the more you read the more boring becomes the story.

Journalism hurt my head until my wife started borrowing children's picture books.

In those wonderfully skinny volumes was the answer to all things, including storytelling. The picture books are on the shelves next to chairs that are too tiny for an adult. You pick a book because it has a good picture on the front and a title you can understand. You read about a pink alligator who is standing at the edge of the river and is afraid of getting his feet wet but wants to get to the other side. What a story. You know what is happening. You feel for the alligator. You are part of the life of an alligator. And lying on the floor near you is a three-year-old who can't read a word and who is mesmerized by a story of a monkey who is learning to peel bananas but drops the peel and his father slips on it. There is going to be trouble in monkey land.

Little kids who are taken to the library march over to the kid's section and pick out their own picture books. They know what's good. They read two or three without looking up. Then they walk out with stacks under their arms. They are thrilled. They are proud. They know the stories and will read them over and over.

Put the same kid in front of a television and you get non-blinking, non-motion, non-remembering tiny consumers who after two hours of TV can only say: "I want Frosted Icy Pops, now on sale for $2.99."

I am not smart enough to write children's books so I stick with television. But from the moment I started reading picture books television changed for me. I just looked for a pink alligator afraid to cross the river or someone planting daffodils in February. Finding life's adventures is simple. Look for someone who is happy or amazed or frightened or grinning and ask them to share a few of their moments. Presto, that's all there is to it.

And I made up new rules for television; they also apply to life.

1. Everything works.
2. Continuity (very big in television) is for wimps.
3. Any kid who stands in front of the camera gets on television. (No kids left on the cutting room floor.)
4. Good people make good stories.
5. The most important rule of all: Repeat rule number one.

If you believe number one, it will work—in television and, with less difficulty, in life.

2

So What Was Wrong with Today?

Something good will happen. I know it will. Rule number one. Forget the fact that I have only three minutes to go before I get home and I can't talk about the fines because that is not the kind of story that will make a pleasant evening.

It is not my job to return my wife's books. She never asks me to do that but I volunteer because I am out all day and I pass libraries all over the place and it is so easy for me to drop them off. Except I forget. And then my wife puts the groceries in the trunk and says loud words which boil down to I will never again be allowed to return any books and the nice librarians are not going to allow her to take out more books which will result in her kids not getting any stories read to them which will result in the demise of all civilization. And it will be my fault.

Always the next day I promise to take more books back. But they wind up in my trunk, too, and in short I help support the nationwide library system with overdue fines and also shorten the time left for man and womankind to survive.

But on this particular evening I was not feeling bad about the
fines. I was feeling bad because I had not found anything during
the entire day that was neat or funny or uplifting or memorable
and happy. Every day I look for something like that, something
like a good children's story.

I learned that from Reilly. He was a child who believed he
would catch a fish even if he was just using a stick and a string
and a paper clip. He said anyone would get what they wanted if
they believed they would get it. "But you have to really believe it,"
he added.

That was the boy and the story that changed my life. After I
met Reilly I started to believe every day that I would find something good. It is like stamp collecting or downloading tunes
except it does not cost anything. If I am working I put the good
thing on television. I am lucky. I am able to share the things that
are out there with others.

But on days that I am not working I still look for something,
like searching for gold, something of value that I can enjoy by
myself or share with one or two others if I happen to meet one
or two others. The stories of good people are collectibles that
you can't buy on eBay. They are always out there if you look hard
enough and if you believe you will find them. Just ask Reilly.

Except I now have only two minutes left on my way back from
the library. But I believe I will find it, I said to the windshield. I
talk a lot to my windshield and anything beyond it. Like Reilly
says, I believe. But I have only four blocks to go before I turn off
the road and will be home, and it is just about dark and, face it, it
is not possible to always find something good. Not always. That's
not the way life works.

And then the kangaroo crossed the road. Right there, right in
front of me.

"He did it. My god, he did it."

I was talking to the windshield. I was shouting at the windshield and things beyond it.

Then I saw something better than a kangaroo. The old elephant now had a baby. "Holy mackerel. Reilly, bless you. You did it. You really did it. Actually you didn't do it. Someone else did it. But you told me to look for it."

I said all this to the windshield and the dashboard and I felt like I was flying—not going fast, just elevating off the ground.

The deer crossing signs on Mount Seymour Parkway are created by Cameron Stewart, a civil servant working in the sign shop at the North Vancouver District works yard. The yard is not known for its creativity but his signs have become famous around the world. I know that for sure because I, and probably you, have gotten emails from friends in England and America and Australia with pictures that say "Deer Crossing" with a picture of a camel or an elephant.

I write back to my friends and say, "Hey, those pictures are from here and they are made by this neat guy who wanted to be an artist but wound up working for the government. Like all civil servants he was given work orders to fulfil but like all happy, creative people he added a drop of genius to the orders. He mixed imagination with the road signs. "Slow Down, Deer Crossing." "Wait, did I just see that right? That was a picture of a camel on a deer crossing sign." The next one had an elephant.

Cameron cheers up thousands of drivers in North Vancouver and millions of email senders around the world.

But his pictures had been up for several years and everything, like sit-coms and TV personalities who are there too long without changing and growing and improving, can grow invisible. That is life. Cameron's signs were becoming unnoticed. Sure we have the most wonderful signs in the world but, like, so? Big deal.

Been there, seen that. Oh hum, a camel warning of deer. We are such demanding creatures.

And then, only three blocks from my home, I see a rhino with a red nose telling drivers to be careful about deer. First a kangaroo, then a rhino—with a red nose. I have never seen deer on that road but now I've seen a red-nosed rhino, and I have a story to tell.

And better than both of them is a baby elephant. My wife likes babies and now there is a cute little thing with its mother on a road where deer are now safe. I can't wait to get home with the news.

See, it is clear. Rule Five is true. Or is it Reilly who is right? Or is it simply the faith in Rule Five—everything works—and the belief that what Reilly said is all you need? Or, even more simply, if you believe things will work, they will.

I turned off the street and the weight of the world was gone. There was something good out there. Reilly and Cameron had saved the day and the night and my faith and everything, and that's a lot to save. And if I hadn't gone to the library I would not have seen the elephant's new baby or the kangaroo or the rhino with the red nose.

I got home and told my wife I had just seen an elephant and her baby, and a rhino with a red nose and a kangaroo.

"That's nice, dear," she said. "Next time I'll return the books."

But I know secretly it made her happy. She would never let on. She went back to her homework pretending she was not as excited as I was, but she was, even if she was shaking her head.

And that's the way a good children's story would end. My wife would make believe she was not thrilled as she went back to her books. But on the next page there would be a picture in which you could peek at her face and she would be smiling.

Score one for Reilly.

That's all there is to having a life that brings you enjoyment every day. In the last book I told you how Reilly, who was nine years old when I met him and autistic, taught me that you simply believe that things will work and they will.

If you haven't tried it yet, it's not too late. It doesn't matter if you think that simply believing that things will work out the way you want them to will actually make them work out the way you want them to is impossible. It doesn't matter at all because it does work and it is possible—like choosing which dress to wear to a party. I learned about dresses from people who wear dresses and they say it is impossible to pick the right one for a party. That is true, unless they believe in Rule Number One.

Also, by believing I would not be sick, I have not been sick. (A major medical emergency where part of my insides was removed doesn't count.) That is seven years without being sick.

Jacquie McIndoe, the editor in the newsroom who made fun of me when I told her that to cure her cold she just had to say she wasn't sick—and believe it—has not been sick for a year. She still makes fun of me, but she has not been sick.

She still won't admit that believing you won't be sick is the best medicine. But I suspect that when she is not feeling well she says, secretly, "I feel fine." She jokes about that. She says, jokingly, that she believes she will not be sick. Then she gets through the day, feeling fine. I know; I look at her and she looks good, even when someone in the next edit room is sneezing and groaning. But again, she won't admit it seriously because then she would have to say, "Yes, it works." And she can't do that because she is a hard-nosed editor who has seen tens of thousands of stories where people are not what they pretend to be. And she has seen other stories about those who get caught up in the new religion of suddenly believing in something and they go overboard with it. She is way beyond that. She will only say she feels good because she's been lucky.

I add, you are not kidding.

By believing I would have a good day, I have had good days. My furnace broke down, my refrigerator stopped working, my favourite uncle died, and those were not good days. But when I got a new furnace I learned the old one was probably going to kill me with escaping poisonous gas. That was good to learn.

And I discovered I had not defrosted my frost-free, never-needs-defrosting refrigerator for ten years and it only had to be unplugged for a day and it worked again after all the ice that was not supposed to be jamming the vents was defrosted.

And I remembered the days when I was young and my mother would send me to my uncle and aunt and their eight kids who lived in the country so I could get away from the city. I spent a long time on the phone with my aunt who had been married for seventy-three years. I told her some of the best days of my life were those I spent with her and my uncle. She cried. She said I made her feel better. I did not take away the pain, of course not. But good stories help ease it.

And some day I believe I will return library books on time. But that takes a profound belief and even with Reilly I do not think I am ready for that elevated status yet. But *someday* I will leave the library without paying a fine. I know it—just not today.

3

The One Simple Trick to a Perfect Day

And now that we have the problems of life conquered, I would like to move on and tell you how to guarantee a good day, every day.

It is always good when you get something new. One of the rules of advertising is to put "NEW" on as many packages as you can. You cannot buy a laundry soap, the old reliable never-changing laundry soap, without seeing NEW on the label.

The human race loves NEW. It is an observable fact. The main floor of basically every department store on earth is devoted to women. At the entrance is the cosmetic department, in which every woman is looking for something NEW.

Most men don't care much about clothing. The men's department is at the back of the store. But go into an auto parts or hardware store: My Lord! The Newest Screwdriver. The Newest Gas Line Anti-Clog Solution. The Newest Rag to wipe off windshields. Men are as easy to sell to as women. Just give them bug repellent instead of lipstick. Of course they will say they are just looking at hubcaps while they are waiting for their wives who are shopping. They themselves are not shopping.

"Hey, Harry, did you see this new compressor? I could use a compressor."

"What for?"

"I don't know, but life would be good if I had a compressor. Especially a new one with newer high compression."

So since we all love to get something new, I am giving you something to look for that will make your life as good as it has made mine. It is a list with just one thing on it: Look for something new. That's all. And while you are at it, make it something Good as well as new. Good with a capital G. Look for something that will knock your socks off, or at least make you smile.

That is my entire outlook and my entire advice. In the last book I said you could have anything you wanted if you really wanted it and believed you would get it. Honest, it never fails.

But if you say phooey to that, if you think positive thinking is not in your field of thought, then I have another suggestion that will work just as well. Remember rule number one. Everything works. This is simple and practical. And on top of it you don't have to say to your friends that you know things will turn out good because you believe they will. That old cornball belief is crazy—if you don't believe it. And if you don't believe it, it will not work. Of course, on the other hand, in truth it does work—without fail.

But if you are afraid of changing your life for the better just by believing, I'll give you this easy way out, and it works just as well. It's something you can do and you don't have to worry about your friends laughing at you.

Go out and find something good. Go find something to tell someone about. "Hey, Harry, I saw this little old lady today and she was going to be hit by a speeding car but this guy raced out and grabbed her and pulled her to safety. It was the neatest thing. He was like Superman. Let's have another beer."

"Did you really see that?"

"No, but I did see a little old lady acting like she was lost in the middle of the street and a young girl came by and helped her to the curb."

"So why didn't you say that in the first place?"

"Because I didn't think you would care, so I made the story better."

"You're an idiot. I like the real story. Here's your beer, and here's to nice young girls."

Look for something good, something you can talk about, something you can share, or remember and tell someone a week later. A good story does not grow old. And a good story makes you feel good.

I am not saying you have to DO something good yourself. That would be raising the bar a bit too high. Next thing you know everyone would be doing something good and the magazines and Oprah would pick up the trend and suddenly there would be the right way and the wrong way of doing something good. There would be TV shows with everyone doing good things and there would be competitive Good Doing and the loser would have to do even better and soon we would have wars over who is doing the best good. I'm not saying go out and change the world. Knowing the record of humanity we would surely wreck it.

I'm just saying go out and find something good that you notice or hear about. Put some effort into it. Forget your smartphone and iPod and look around. Search for the grimy, evil-looking kid who holds the door open for a man with a walker. Look for the little girl who puts her mittens on the stick arms of a snow-man. Take a picture of the guy who is building inukshuks along the Olympic walkway near Science World, if he is still there. He was crawling around the shoreline for five months building little stone men and making the world a more interesting place.

That's all. Find one good, oddball, sweet, funny, neat, friendly, positive, pretty or mind-blowing thing a day and your life will be good. That's all it takes. That is the whole secret. That one thing will make you feel good. And when you tell someone else about it they will feel good. And at that moment you will have made the world a better place and, unlike the man with stone figures by the seawall, you will not have had to do any strenuous lifting.

It's not hard, and it works.

I'll give you an example.

The Christmas Present

4

This is one of those children's stories that is perfect. It has poop in it, a bathroom word that kids love to say but are forbidden to utter, and a twist that makes five-year-olds laugh and know that life really does turn out to be backwards.

The neatest thing that happened to me over last Christmas was someone let their dog poop on my grass. It was a pile of poop: a thick, black manicotti-looking pile overlapping itself. Forgive me, but it is important to know this.

"Darn," I said.

Actually I said something else. I saw it when I came home from work. "Not just before Christmas," I said to myself. "It's bad anytime of the year, but especially now when people are supposed to be good."

It was on the side of my house where I cannot see. There are no windows on that side and dog walkers are on their honour. Most are nice, but one got a "Darn you to heck" from me. I did not have time to clean it up that night.

I saw it again from my car when I drove off the next morning. "Darn."

23

Rotten people. Awful, rotten people, whoever it was. I fumed all day. I was angry because I could not see who was doing it and whoever it was knew I could not see them. And I described it to myself again: it was black and piled with those coils of poop that are ugly.

I drove home that night and drove past it again, and again said, "Darn."

I said other things, too, but this is family reading, and it doesn't matter because you know what those other things were. You have said them also, when someone let their dog go on your grass and slipped away into the night.

I got some cardboard and wrote, "Merry Christmas to you, too!!!!!"

I like to be subtle.

And then I wrote, "You give a bad name to all dog owners."

It was not exciting writing, but it would get the point across.

I taped the sign to a metal pole and got a hammer and went out to the side of my house. I would hammer it in the ground right next to the poop so that the poopster would feel embarrassed and others would see it and hate the poopster too, because they knew they might be looked at as a suspect. There was Christmas music playing in my house, but I wanted to spread the hate all around and fertilize the guilt and get my revenge.

Don't mess with my grass.

I stood over it. I looked down, closely. There on the ground under my eyes was a black leather glove with the fingers overlapping themselves. Someone probably put it there to keep it safe after they found it lying in the street.

Would you like to buy a sign that says, "Merry Christmas to you, too!!!!"?

I am letting it go cheap.

5

The Reality of Telling that Story

You are sitting at the kitchen table. There is a lull in the conversation because your six-year-old has suddenly decided to take a bite of dinner instead of complaining about it. Her older brother is staring at his plate seeing the beautiful face of a new girl he met today. Your wife, or husband, is exhausted because you have not had to deal with kids who don't appreciate you and a mate who has nothing to contribute to the conversation.

"Say, you remember that pile of poop that was on the grass?"

"Awwww, Dad (Mom) that's disgusting," says the older brother. "And I said I would pick it up. I just haven't gotten around to it."

"But…" you try to say.

"But nothing, now I can't eat," he says.

"But a funny thing…" you try to say.

"Honestly, dear!" (That's your soulmate of course who is suddenly defensive, offensive, offended and annoyed all at once just because you are trying to tell a joke that concerns poop.) "Do you have to talk about that at the table?"

"But…"

"Daddy (Mommy),"—the six-year-old is ready to pounce. "We're not allowed to say poop. If we say poop in school we get demerit points and that's bad. So I never say poop. But YOU said poop. So can I tell the teacher that you said poop? Please?"

"I just wanted to say…" says the storyteller who is trying to bring joy to the family.

"Not now."

"But."

"PLEASE. Not NOW."

"It was…"

"I don't care what it was, if you say another word about that now I'm leaving the table."

(Something similar to this really happened, different family, different generations. Same words.)

Telling a story is not always easy. You want to lighten the evening, but you're not allowed to open your mouth.

"It was a glove," you blurt. You can't say it, you have to blurt it before anyone gets a chance to get up and walk away.

"What was a glove?"

"The…" But you can't say it.

However, the six-year-old gets it.

"You mean the poop wasn't poop, it was a glove?"

"Sweetheart, you're so smart."

"Then why were you so mad about it for two days? If it was just a glove why didn't you pick it up?"

"Because I didn't know. I didn't look."

"Why didn't you look," says the older brother who has found that you have made a mistake, which counterbalances his last one hundred slip-ups and so this has made his night.

"You always tell me to be careful and keep my eyes open," he says.

"But I was just making a joke. See, I got fooled. I thought the poop was…"

"Can I say poop now?" says little sister.

"No, you can't say poop in school. You can only say poop at home," you say, instantly realizing you have just stepped into the figurative equivalent of the same.

"No, she can't," interjects, firmly, your soulmate. "What are you teaching these children?"

"I'm just trying to be funny."

"Poop is funny," says older brother.

"It is not funny at the dinner table," says soulmate.

"It's still funny," you say, "like it's a good story to tell to your family. I read in a book that if you tell one good story a day your life will be better."

Six eyes staring at you. Six unblinking eyes.

"You mean…" says soulmate.

"What are you saying?" says older brother.

"What are you saying, Daddy (Mommy)?" says little girl.

"You are doing this all for yourself?" says soulmate.

"No," says you, super emphatically, defensively, suddenly realizing that it just might be selfish. "I was just trying to give you all a laugh."

"Suppose we didn't think it was very funny?" continues soulmate.

"But I read that if you tell a story your life will be better. And everyone's will be better," you add quickly, hoping that was in the book, too.

"Well, you go tell anyone who writes such nonsense they are not helping us. And to bring up poop at a time when I am trying to get our son to eat his mashed spinach is not a wise move."

"Sorry."

The next day at breakfast someone, while grabbing a piece of toast on the way out and not saying goodbye as usual, suddenly says, "That was a very funny story you told last night." That was older brother.

He spoke, you think.

He comes back. "Hope you don't mind if I tell that story at school."

"My goodness gosh. It worked," you think.

"Which story?" you ask. "The glove or the discussion at the table."

"The table, of course," he says, looking at you as if you don't understand anything. "That's the only thing that's funny."

Doesn't matter. The story worked.

Ziggy and the Stones

6

In France they saw him and I know more people talked about him than about some of the athletes. The same in Germany and Japan. "The Olympics are great, but I saw a story on this guy building stone men. It was beautiful," said a tourist from Germany.

"You really did?"

"Yes, I saw it in Germany and now I am here and he is here. This is wonderful," said the tourist.

The same in the US where everyone was disappointed about the last hockey game; they said, "I saw this neat story of a guy who was doing something for everyone."

Every reporter was trying to get one more story, something that was fun, interesting and easy to report on. And many of the thousands of reporters covering the games walked by Ziggy and said, "Oh, you beautiful answer to a prayer."

Along the seawall, a little north of Science World, Ziggy was kneeling among the rocks by the edge of the water turning an ugly patch of ground into a make-believe world. He was building little inukshuks, each about the size of your forearm.

Some had heads, some arms, some both. Some were just piles

29

of rocks on top of rocks, but neatly designed piles. They were not gravity defying. I once met a homeless man who could make a jagged twenty-pound granite boulder balance on top of a one-pound rock connected by nothing but a fingernail sliver of stone. That was art.

What Ziggy was doing was civic improvement.

"I am Ziggy. You ask who I am, I am Ziggy. I am unemployed Polish immigrant. I had nothing to do so I made this look better."

He tilted back his baseball hat with his gloved hand. The fingers in the gloves had worn away.

"I have been on television around the world. People come here and tell me they saw me in England. Now they see me for real."

He was so proud. He had started with four small rocks at the edge of False Creek, just above the high tide mark. He made them into a pint-sized inukshuk. Then he built another, and another. At night some rowdy kids—who else do you blame—knocked them down.

The next day Ziggy put them up again and added dozens more. By the end of the first week passing visitors had become the protectors of the stones. Anyone trying to knock them down was browbeaten by people who saw something that needed protecting and they took on the job.

Ziggy could stop his rebuilding program and get on with new construction, expanding the seaside town of Ziggyville.

"I should not have lost my job. I am in maintenance and I am good maintenance worker," he said. "But here, this is my medicine. It is better than drinking or cursing."

I don't know why he lost his job. I could only follow some of what he was saying, but that is about average for most people, including myself. We start by talking about the weather and then go into our problems and then some of the details of them while our listener has stopped listening and is trying to interrupt with his own problems. So Ziggy was really no different from most, except he was making things look better.

By the end of the first week of the Olympics he had made hundreds of little stone friends, and reporters were almost lining up to do stories about him. I did one on the reporters.

By the middle of the second week he had a thousand stone friends and millions of TV admirers. Several people asked me for his phone number, which I gave them. They talked with him about a job, but nothing came of it. That is sad. That is life. Maybe they just did not have any opening for someone to make mini inukshuks.

During the end of the last week of the games I would wander down to the seawall at night. The endless crowd had made a new, unofficial path. Instead of staying between the beer tents of Molson's and various provinces, the swarm of visitors detoured through a side gate and walked on the path looking down at the stones.

"Amazing." "Can't believe it." "You should see it in the daytime."

In the daylight the little stone army went from the water at the edge of the parking lot under the Sky Train (don't worry if you have no idea where that is) to the Edgewater Casino (same thing). It was a long, long way. I tried counting them, but it was silly. Others tried. Maybe 5,000, maybe 10,000.

I saw Ziggy one last time after the beer tents had been taken down and the athletes had gone. He was beaming.

"I did all this, and I am Ziggy."

And then he disappeared. He told me he was living in a rooming house, but had just moved in and was moving out. He said he would be leaving town and then he said he would be staying.

Time, tide, wind and those rotten kids finally got the better of his little people. A few weeks later they, like Ziggy, had disappeared. The rocks were still there, but they were back where they had started. Their life was gone.

On the other hand, for one brief shining moment something had happened. Ziggy gave us something along with himself. It was sad that nothing came out of it in the end, but it would have been much sadder if nothing had ever been there.

One man making many stories and each of them beginning with: "You won't believe this."

That is something.

7

Billy and the Horse

It is easy to prove that everyone is connected. Listen to any story about anyone and it will lead to someone else.

"What? Miss Johnson was your grandmother? She was my grade three teacher!"

Suddenly two grown women who had met casually only because their kids were in the same class became an instant family. Their kids, one boy and one girl, who would grow up as friends and then marry, would tell the story of how they were destined to be together because of Miss Johnson, whom they never met.

Every day, everywhere, something like that is happening.

"I have an idea," said Dave McKay, the cameraman. He was shooting the demolition of a housing area at 33rd and Main, and some construction worker told him they'd found something in an old peanut butter jar.

Old peanut butter jar? You don't get more romantic than that. That was a gift from story heaven.

"What was in it?" I asked.

"Don't know. I didn't get a chance to ask and then he was gone."

We drove to 33rd and Main. Any lead on any story, just like any potential opportunity in life, must be followed. Any suggestions you ignore will not increase your bank account or your life. It is like a great observation by the Great One, Wayne Gretzky. "The pucks you don't shoot won't go in the net."

You don't need much more philosophy in life beyond that.

We drove to 33rd and Main. It is a four-block area that once had more than two hundred families in it and was Vancouver's oldest public housing. It was built to provide rental apartments for war vets who had returned but found nowhere they could afford to live.

It was called "the projects" in Vancouver. The first time I heard that I thought they were kidding.

"The projects are slums twenty stories high that have hallways filled with scary, loitering teenagers and urine," I said. "At least that's what they were in New York."

"Well, this is our projects," said whomever I was with that day.

Between the buildings was grass and trees and across the street is one of the most beautiful parks in the world.

I brought visiting New Yorkers to 33rd and Main and told them to close their eyes.

"You are going to see Vancouver's projects. You are going to see social housing. You are going to see how tough life is here. Open your eyes."

"My God!"

That was the first response by a friend who had lived in the New York projects as a kid.

"My God!"

That was his second comment.

He remembered the five locks on his door and his mother giving him two sets of money when he went out to get milk. One was in his pocket and he would give it up to the kid robbers who would grab him after he got to the sidewalk. The other was in his sock so he could buy the milk.

He remembered the concrete walls and steel gratings over the windows that made looking outside at the rows of other buildings impossible. He remembered the sirens. There were always sirens and they were always racing to the projects.

"My God!"

He was looking at enough grass-covered space between the buildings to hit a ball with a bat. He was looking at the three stories and then a roof, not twenty stories topped with tar where you would go in the summertime to try to find fresh air. He was looking across the street at Queen Elizabeth Park, which was the playground for the kids when they got tired of the swings inside the projects. And he was looking at Nat Bailey Stadium, where you could watch minor league professional baseball for less cost than a large latte.

"My…"

"I know," I said.

"I want to live here."

But time passed and the city knocked down the buildings in late 2009. Land values were up and condos could be built where projects used to stand and the city could sell the condos at sky-high prices and make a profit. The displaced folks were moved into other housing across the street—not as much grass, but spanking new apartments. There were protests against the demolition, there always are by those who feel they have to protest. You can't and should not stop them. As long as they don't cover their faces they have a right to say change is wrong. And then change happens and thirty years later the protesters have grown older and think that the new crop of young protesters are silly. It almost always happens.

What will happen at the old projects is more tax-paying

people will move into the condos, which will pay for more social housing and integrate the poorer with the richer, and hopefully some of the poorer will one day say, "Hey, I want to be like them." And instead of complaining that they are not like those rich people, some of them will try to be like them, which will make life for them much better.

Back to Dave the cameraman, who had heard that someone found something in one of the old buildings.

"Something?"

"I don't know what. Something in a peanut butter jar."

That was sort of like a comment in 1856: "I heard there's gold in the Fraser River."

"Where's that?"

"I don't know, but if there's gold there we should go."

And so British Columbia was born. Folks came to get the gold. The story is in previous books but in short this land was filled with mostly Americans looking for yellow stones, and the head of the Hudson's Bay trading post, James Douglas, told Queen Victoria that she'd better do something quickly or this lovely land would be claimed by America.

The good Queen signed a piece of paper that made it part of England. That was close. And she sent the paper back on a sailing ship that took forever to get here. If that ship had sunk in a storm or even been delayed by a side trip to a warm Caribbean island this land containing Vancouver and Prince George and Watson Lake would be another star on the Stars and Stripes.

We drove to 33rd and Main, and so began this story.

There was almost nothing left. Of the scores of buildings that were there a few weeks ago there were only three standing, and they were behind a high fence with large signs that said: "Don't Enter" and "Construction Site." Another sign said, "You Are Not Allowed In Here, No Matter What." Creative prohibition.

"You think that applies to us?" Dave asked me.

We tried a security guard.

"Can't you read?"

"Who told you about the peanut butter jar?" I asked Dave.

"A big guy."

We drove around the block and there was a big guy standing on the street. That is plain luck.

"Try him," said Dave to me. Dave uses few words.

"Hello, we are from Global."

"I know," said the big guy. "I was wondering when you would come after I told your friend about the peanut butter jar."

How did he happen to be standing there? That's one of life's mysteries. The fact that he was the safety officer and it was his job to stand outside the site and make sure things are safe had nothing to do with it. He was there and we needed him and there was something magical about that. At least I believe it.

"Do you have the peanut butter jar?" I asked.

"Well, yes, and no," he said. "It is in the site office, which is behind the fence, which now belongs to the Canada Housing and Mortgage Corporation and I don't know if I am allowed to take it out or if you are allowed to go in and see it."

Problems. Always problems.

But solutions, always solutions.

"I'll call the superintendent," he said.

He did. Dave took a picture of him calling, because you never know when something, anything, will become something else. It is a rule of life: Never ignore anything, especially big or small things.

"He said," said the big man, "he's not authorized to give permission."

Already I felt something big coming on. Something exciting makes things grow: a tree from an acorn, a chick from an egg—

you know the rest, a story from a phone call.

His name was Brad Morrison, and he said he would try someone in the government agency overseeing the operation. He called.

"No," Brad told us. "The government agent can't give me authority to show items found inside the site."

Of course not. Who would expect anything but a bureaucratic shuffling off of decision making? Decision makers in places of authority will do anything but make a decision. It might cost them their authority.

We wanted to see a peanut butter jar and there was no telling how many levels of bureaucracy that would take. To raise taxes the government only has to make an announcement, but to see an old peanut butter jar, that would mean someone would have to give permission and who would take such a risk?

Some day, far down the long road of civil service advancement, someone may ask someone who wants to be the head of something if he or she has ever given permission for a peanut butter jar to be displayed publicly without personally examining the jar and without having an investigation into the possible hazards of showing one brand of peanut butter over another and the health hazards involved in keeping a jar that long and the person will be passed over for someone who protected the privacy of the jar.

No kidding.

Brad made six more calls seeking permission to show us a peanut butter jar and a picture that he said was in it, but no one would give it to him. Dave kept the camera on him.

I was thinking this might be a good story—the Watergate Jar cover-up. If you do not get that allusion, it is to one of the biggest political cover-ups in modern history, involving Richard Nixon, the President of the United States. The peanut butter jar was following the same path.

When I started as a reporter we were allowed to go anywhere. We, at least in North America, poked into the halls of justice and police buildings and at least were able to try to sneak into businesses to get the stories of greed and corruption.

Then came Watergate, which is a hotel in Washington where skulduggery went on concerning how to get Richard Nixon re-elected. It was illegal skulduggery. Following most things illegal there is a cover-up to hide the illegal stuff.

Then there was a leak to a couple of young reporters about the cover-up from someone who did not like what was going on. When they wrote a story about the cover-up there were more cover-ups to cover up the cover-ups. The cover-ups became more important than the crime because there was a suspicion that the cover-ups went right up to the top guy, who was Richard Nixon, and it would be bad for people to believe that the president was covering up a crime. That would be criminal.

Then Nixon erased some things from an audio tape in his office. Those things are never supposed to be erased. They are part of the permanent record of what goes in the place where the country's fate is decided. But he scrubbed eighteen minutes of something. Whoops. That was criminal.

More leaks dripped out and what do you know, Nixon resigned. His last words were "I am not a crook." You don't often hear such a powerful defence as that from a US president.

What should have followed would have been an attempt to make leaders and helpers of leaders honest. That would have been nice.

What actually followed was the human reaction: Information will be controlled; leaks will be shut off; dirty laundry will never been seen.

In one generation, that's my simple and not long lifetime, reporting has become a closed door. From the police you get a spokesperson. From the government, a spokesperson. From business, the same. From the church, a spokesperson. From ICBC, from Terasen Gas, from YVR, from the hospitals, from the teachers union, a spokesperson. I am in no way saying the leaders of those and other bodies are doing illegal things. A spokesperson is a wise move.

A spokesperson makes it easy for corporations and politicians to control the output of news. It makes it convenient for reporters. They don't have to work. But for the public, it is terrible. Every bit of information is funnelled through one person. You cannot talk to the people involved. You cannot ask questions from someone who was actually at the scene of the disaster or who is uncovering the case of the crashed and written-off cars that are being resold. You only get the spokesperson.

All facets of society, even the social workers and the charity groups that help the poor and the outcasts (and I love those groups) have built walls around themselves. They not only keep out reporters, they keep out you, because you only hear one version, the official version, of what is going on. Many reporters now spend most of their working lives trying to figure out what spokespeople actually meant.

My only suggestion is don't trust what you hear, especially not the official version. A rule of thumb is when an official person says something is "Up," you should anticipate that half of it is actually "Down," and going lower.

So when Brad was up against the stone wall surrounding the peanut butter jar I thought that might be a good essay, sort of, on what I just said.

Then he said, "Just follow me. It's only a peanut butter jar."

Brad is a big man. But people who step over the walls of bureaucracy and make up their own minds are truly big.

We followed, through an opening in the fence and past the

security guard who had told us we could not enter, but now it was okay because we were "with him."

We followed to the one remaining building, which was the site office, and waited outside.

Brad came out. He carried a Squirrel Peanut Butter jar and a piece of paper and a photo. "These were in the jar," he said showing us the paper and the picture.

This was gold, true gold, pure gold. This was a story I could tell forever, even if I didn't know what it was. But it was something from the past that was here and now. It was not just a jar and picture and paper, it was something that made the then of the past and the now of today one thing in one time and one place.

Okay, I know that this is all Main Street philosophy, but it is pretty cool. You look at an old photo of your grandparents when they were children and know that their parents were looking at the same pictures and thinking what beautiful kids they have and they hoped they would have a good life.

They did not know about you and you do not know them, but you are as connected to that picture as they were. They looked at the photo and touched it. You look at it and touch it. You know what you feel.

"I can't believe those are our grandparents."

Imagine what their parents felt. "I can't believe those are our children."

At times like that there is no past and no future. It is forever Now.

That of course explains eternity, at least to me.

The photo in the jar: A young boy with a cowboy hat sitting on a pony. Written on the back of the picture was: "Billy, age 8."

It was a story suitable for framing or telling or television. This was a keeper. Billy, age eight, sitting on a pony. Billy with a cowboy hat on his head and a smile below it. Who was Billy? We had no idea. We had no idea of how the picture came to be. It was just a moment in a jar, and I thought it would have a lifespan on TV of a few minutes. I am so often so wrong.

As soon as the story was on the air hundreds, maybe thousands, of people around the province sat up. "I know that horse. I sat on it. I have that picture."

The tidal wave of recognition went across the land, including on the anchor desk.

When the story was over, Wayne Cox the weatherman said, "I have that same picture. Some guy brought that horse around one summer and had kids lining up for pictures."

He said he remembered there was only one stirrup on the side where the camera could see.

By five after seven the phone board was clogging with calls of those who remembered, including Sgt. Peter Thiessen, the spokesperson of the RCMP. What I said before about spokespersons does not apply to him.

The next day we were running around getting the stories of people who were grown now and with children and some with grandchildren who had sat on that same pint-sized horse. The story was the same wherever we went. The little steed was brought into a neighbourhood in the back of a pickup truck, unloaded on a street corner, and the kids lined up.

"Go home, get your money and I'll take your picture on a real western horse," said the man holding the cowboy hat.

Who could pass up this? The quarters poured in. The pictures were delivered and more than fifty years later they were rediscovered. What more wonderful thing could there be?

Many who called us were at work in schools and hospitals and offices. A few were grandmothers at home watching the littlest of little ones. Everyone had been desperately searching through closets and drawers for their old pictures. And everyone seemed to be in roughly the same age group, still a half dozen years from retirement but none older and none younger.

That was not hard to figure out. The horse came around for a few years, and then no more.

But where was Billy? No calls. No hints. No leads. The perfect story would be that after he sat on the horse he set his life in a heroic direction and from that moment on he wanted to be something, anything, all because of the horse. We envisioned him to have been a business executive or a real cowboy or something, because you want those you have met as kids to succeed in life.

But as time passed we assumed he had died or moved away. Who could not know we were searching for him? He must have friends or neighbours who would have seen it and recognized him as a kid. There must have been.

A week later someone called. A low voice, like it was a secret. "I know Bill."

"Bill who?"

"Bill the guy on the horse. You know, the guy."

"Of course." I was excited. "Do you know him?"

"Yeah," he whispered.

"Is this a secret?"

"Could be. I don't know if he wants anyone to know."

"To know what?"

"To know him. He's kind of private."

Oh, God, I am thinking. A kid on a horse has turned into a cloak with a dagger.

"Here's a number. It might not work. Don't tell him I called."

"I don't even know who you are."

"Good." He hung up.

I called the number. "Yeah?"

I told him who I was and asked if he was the guy on the horse.

"What horse?" he asked. "And why do you want to know?"

"To take your picture."

"What for?

"Okay, let's get down to business," I said, as if I was Jack Webb on Dragnet. "Did you ever sit on a horse and have your picture taken and put the picture in a peanut butter jar and hide it in the housing project up near 33rd and Main?"

That was simple.

"What horse?" said the voice.

"Never mind." I gave up.

"Yes, I had a picture taken. Someone in the beer parlour told me I was on TV, but I didn't see it."

"Would you like to see it?" There was friendliness in my voice. I know it was there because I told myself to put it there.

He said yes and told me his mother lived near the old projects in a new projects that was fancy and clean and better than the old projects.

We arranged to meet her and her son at a bus stop at 36th and Main. Billy's mother was there first and she was standing in the cold, shivering.

"You can wait inside. I'll call you when Billy gets here," I said to her.

"No," she said. "I want to see my Billy. I remember the picture."

She was thin, truly frail, and shaking.

"He said he'd be on the next bus," I said.

But the next bus came, and went. And the one after that came and went. I called the number.

"I can't make it today," said Billy. "My back hurts."

He was going to get it massaged. Welfare has been very good to him.

I looked into the speaker of the phone. I looked really hard.

"Billy," I said very calmly and with a very deep voice. "Listen to me."

"Yeah?"

"Are you listening?"

"Yeah."

"Listen very closely. You are not getting a massage. You are getting on a bus and coming here."

"But."

"Billy. Listen. There are no 'buts.' Get on the bus and come. Do not stop. Get off the bus when you see your mother. Do not miss the next bus."

I have a rule, never interfere with reality. Just show it the way it is—except when you have to. Sometimes you have to grab hold of reality and shape it the way you think it should be. You might be wrong, but you are not going to get a second chance.

Two buses later Billy got off the bus. His hair was straggly, and so were his clothes. His mother was smiling.

"Hug your mother," I said. He did.

I have another rule. Never tell anyone what to do—except when you have to. Sometimes someone needs a little prompting to get going in the direction you think is right. That might be wrong, but you do it anyway because you can't let it go in the opposite direction. In short, make up your own rules as you need them.

He hugged his mother and she said, "Oh, Billy, I knew you would come."

We walked to the demolition site and met Brad who was waiting with the old photo. He jokingly held it up to Bill's face to see if it was the same person.

"Perfect," he said.

It wasn't. Billy had aged. The cowboy had tied up his horse at the saloon and walked inside and stayed there. Such is life.

"Do you remember getting your picture taken on the horse?" I asked.

"No," said Billy.

The saloon steals the memory.

"Well, here's your picture," said Brad. And Billy and his mother left, walking together. "I'll put it in a frame for you," she said.

I could not hear what he said, if he said anything. He was too far away. In truth, he was very far away.

Not all stories end the way you hope. They end their own way. That's what makes them stories, real stories.

But then, surprise, a prize was waiting. The story would end at a different time and place. The next day I got a phone call. I want things to turn out well, and if you want something badly enough, as Reilly says, it will happen. It just did not happen with Billy. Or maybe it did. His mother now has the picture framed on her wall.

But the phone call was from a couple in Burnaby who said they knew the horse. In fact, his name was Major and he had spent two winters with them.

The next day I was at their home. They were Robert and Les Lee Lowe who have lived in the same house for almost fifty years. They once had orchards and pasture but the city grew and now they had a backyard, but with history.

"Would you like some tea?" Les Lee asked me.

"No thank you." I have been taught to be polite and say no.

"Would you like some cookies?"

"No, thank you."

The cameraman, Karl Cassleman, showed up. Karl looks at life as if it is a bowl of wonton and noodle soup with barbecued pork on top, along with potstickers and beer. He sees the day as a party. He jokes and laughs and he also takes pictures. He is an exuberant, neat guy.

"Would you like some cookies," the lady of the house asked Karl.

"Love them," he said.

"And some tea?"

"That goes good with cookies."

I want to get on with the story. I have a deadline. I have needs.

"Would you like to try my fruit cake," Les Lee asked Karl.

He smiled. "That's my favourite."

She took the aluminum foil off her cake.

"I can smell the brandy," said Karl.

I can smell my deadline dying.

"It's rum," said Les Lee, but it was easy to see she was pleased. Someone wanted her fruit cake and knew there was something special in it. That's all you have to do in life to make someone else happy. Appreciate them.

Karl ate the three pieces she cut for him. Then he started taking pictures of the photos of Major the horse while it was in their backyard. He put the camera on their kitchen table and put the photos in front of the lens and pushed the record button and his hand slipped over the aluminum foil and freed another slice of cake for himself.

"You can't do that, Karl," I said.

But I was wrong. He did it, and I looked at the face of our gracious host. He could have taken the whole cake and it would only have made her happier.

What I learned from Karl is: Take off the chains of what you should do and you will free others.

The story of the horse was touching. One fall day in the early 1960s a man knocked on their door and asked if he could leave his horse with them over the winter.

What a different world. Robert said sure. They had a large backyard and already had another horse, also a miniature breed. But the man at the door did not know that.

They kept the horse without asking for a penny or being offered any money.

"He was a little weak when we first got him, but after a while of walking and eating he was fine," said Robert.

They had pictures of their kids riding him and the little horse, named Major, took to their family with horse happiness.

In the spring the man came back and collected Major. He put him in the back of his pickup truck and left. No offer of money even then, and none was expected.

In the fall he came back and left Major again.

"He was very weak," said Les Lee. "One day he lay down on the ground right there." She pointed to a spot behind their back door next to some trees. "And he died."

The hunt for Billy and the horse was over. It woke up memories in so many. No one I talked to knew the name of the horse, which is not surprising because when a horse comes into town and you get your picture taken on it you don't ask the name. You are thrilled. You are given a cowboy hat to wear for two minutes and you are a cowgirl or boy and are riding the range.

Major carried hundreds, maybe thousands, of kids. In the end, he had a comfortable place to lie down and go to sleep.

And Karl ate half the fruit cake, which made the woman who once fed Major very happy.

I suspect that later that day she was on the phone to one or two of her kids who had ridden Major around their backyard and told them about this amazing cameraman who *loved* her cake. It was a good ending to a mystery—a full stomach, a smile and the knowledge that Major was still in hundreds, maybe thousands, of good memories.

Boys and Girls of Summer

8

Dennis had just bought a new baseball glove. I met him on a field in New Westminster but I was confused. A baseball glove takes a couple of years to break in, especially if you are a weekend player. Firstly, it is stiff and hard to catch with. Secondly, it doesn't look like a baseball glove. It needs sweat to soak into its creases and dirt to get rubbed into its back.

A good baseball glove should flop closed or open when it is dropped on the ground, not remain with a preformed pocket. The webbing on a glove should be frayed from rubbing against the bench while you wait for your time at bat. That takes a lot of waiting and a lot of rubbing.

And most of all, a good glove has to have some whisker scratches or even teeth marks from those times in the dugout when the score is tied and it is the bottom of the ninth and the count is full. "Come on, come on, hit the darn thing." Then the pitch, the swing and you drop your glove to your lap when the batter misses, or swing your hands high and scrape the leather against the chain-link fencing at the top of the dugout after that wonderful sound of a bat on a ball.

You know when you get a new glove that you have to work it, and that takes time.

Dennis Buncal got a new glove for this season. He has played all his life; he knows how long it takes to soften the leather. He was 77 when he showed me his new glove.

The others on the Moody Blues were Don, 66 ("I love the game."), Rodah, 64 ("You should come when the other women are playing. I do it because I love it."), Dennis, 77 ("I've played all my life. Why should I stop now?") and Cam, 66 ("This is the first time I've played since I was 16. It feels good.").

There were others in their 60s and 70s, all hitting and fielding. I saw them practising. Their next game would be on the weekend and I would have to miss that. But just swinging their bats and catching and throwing the hitter out was fine to watch.

None of them under 60. One over 80, not here today. Then all of a sudden, I realized I could join them. I was older than some of them and I felt wonderful. I could swing a bat and catch. This is not so remarkable.

What was remarkable was that it was not so remarkable.

When you are in your 20s or 30s, looking at these old folks might give you a chuckle or inspire you. When you are in your 60s or 70s you just get the urge to play ball. That's what made me love them so much.

A few years earlier I ran into a farm team for these folks, although neither the farm team nor the old folks knew about each other. The youngsters had no gloves and no bat, except for the hunk of driftwood they found on the beach.

They also had no knowledge of baseball, except what they had learned in Canada over the past few seasons.

Allen and Rodrigo, both about ten, with a worn tennis ball they had found in a park and the driftwood bat and each other. Honestly, what more do you need?

They were on Sunset Beach when I saw them, one pitching, the other hitting, the pitcher then running because after the hit the pitcher became the fielder, while the batter was running to first base, which was wherever they thought it might be, and the fielder who was the pitcher now running back to tag him out.

The batter, who was now the base runner, was sliding feet first into second base after hitting the ball from first base while the outfielder, who was now charging to second base, made a head-long dive with the ball outstretched. "Safe." "Out." "Safe." "Out."

If I was the umpire there is no way on earth I could have called that play. With a tie it usually goes to the runner, but the pitcher who became the outfielder had no one to throw to so he also became a runner.

"Do over," said Rodrigo.

Brilliant. He will grow up to be a player's agent, making millions.

Rodrigo was from Paraguay. He had been here two years, the same as Allen, who was from Slovakia. Neither had ever heard of baseball, and now they were playing on the sand at Sunset Beach.

Pow. What a hit! But the ball went into the water. They tried to use the bat to reach it, but it was going out further. Then they both took off their shoes and walked out into False Creek. On the next pitch the ball was sopping wet, their legs were covered with sand and then again the hit, the run, the slide and the dive.

That's the way baseball, in fact every sport, was meant to be played. I don't know how we messed it up with so much money and special equipment and rules. But that day in New Westminster and this one at the beach I saw baseball as it was designed to be played: for the fun of it.

9

Front Row to a Picture Book

Okay, watching this one unfold was easy, except for Jackson, who was the main player. It was easy for me when I stopped at a playground because three little boys were playing basketball. What more could I hope for? But the first rule before all other rules is, "Are you their father?"

"Yes, of two, the other's a friend."

Good enough for me. In this time in our space we never, NEVER, talk to or much less tape any kid under the age of obnoxiousness. That would mean teenagers. Anyone younger than that is off limits even if they are being cuter than cute.

"See that?" sez cameraman.

"What?" sez I.

"Cute kids."

"Parent there?"

"Can't see one. Might be. Maybe."

"Then the kids aren't there. Keep going."

"Shame."

"You're not kidding."

That's our world. Because some people have ruined a good thing, that is they have ruined the lives of innocent kids, the rest of us are denied the enjoyment of watching innocent kids. I don't like the people who have done those things for two reasons: one, they have hurt kids, and that's a sin; and two, they have cancelled out hundreds of wonderful stories that would have made the world a better place.

But on this day in this playground somewhere in south Vancouver there were three small kids and a parent. Good.

There was also a basketball, which made it better, and a hoop that was regulation ten feet off the ground, which made it irresistible.

The biggest boy was Jackson, aged six, whose head came up to about the bottom of my ribs. Joshua also six, was a few inches shorter, and Scott, five, was not in the running. He was a full head shorter than Joshua, which left him miles under the rim.

But they had a basketball and were trying as hard as hard could be to get it in the hoop. The major obstacle was that none of them could throw it high enough to reach the hoop, or even the bottom of the backboard.

"Have you ever gotten a basket?" I asked them.

"I have, I got lots," said Scott, the shortest. It is always this way. The one you first count out is the one who counts. There should be a lesson there.

But his scoring was in school and the hoop was only five feet off the ground. That makes the kids feel good, but it's not counting today.

"I got two," said Joshua. "But that was in school, too. This is so high."

They are smart enough to know when they are given an advantage. Kids who can understand that will probably turn out not to take from society but to give to it.

"I've never had a basket," said Jackson. "But I'm going to get one today."

"Would you feel better if you had cheerleaders?" I asked.

"Yuck, no. They are girls," said Jackson.

Suddenly the picture book was nearing publication. Three boys, thinking like boys, taking turns, bouncing the ball and then throwing, one who had never gotten a ball through the hoop and two who had. What would happen on the last page?

"You can do it," said their father, who was in several shots of the camera because we must make sure folks at home feel comfortable. He repeated, "You can do it." That was important. He gave encouragement. He was with them. The littlest of things often count the most.

The game got intense. "Jackson shoots again, and again. Misses."

"Getting tired?" I ask.

He nods. Things are not looking so good. In a good story a bad thing always happens before something good happens—that's what keeps the drama in life and makes kids, and the rest of us, stronger.

"I can't do it," said Jackson. His arms were getting tired. His throws were going lower and lower.

He left the court and sat in a swing. I was sad. He said he would do it, and now, at six, he was letting himself down. Six-year-olds are allowed to do that. But it is harder to become seven if they do.

Scott and Joshua were still throwing the ball, but it did not get halfway up to the hoop. This was not a happy time for me. I was thinking we will go on and find another story, or maybe their father will say they have to go and I could say that the zero-zero-zero game was called on account of lunch.

And then, from nowhere, meaning from behind where I was sitting on a bench, Jackson came running across the court bouncing a kid-sized soccer ball, half the size of their basketball.

He ran, he threw, he missed.

But he did get close. "Neat." "Great." "Almost."

There is nothing like an honest compliment to inspire anyone. Jackson threw again, and hit the rim.

"You can do it. I know you can."

That was me. I know I'm not supposed to interfere with reality, but really, you can take that rule and forgetaboutit.

And then the ball went up, went way up from his hands through the air and arched through the invisible line that separates a good shot from a sigh and went perfectly through the middle of the basket, swish. Of course there was no net and the ball was a quarter the size of the hoop, but I swear it made a swish.

"I did it, I did it!" Jackson shouted. His father patted him on the back. Joshua and Scott gave him high fives. I said, "You saved my day."

Truly he did. When the story went back to the anchor desk, Chris and company were all smiles. The best grins are involuntary. They are the ones that glow. I still smile when I remember it happening. My bet is you were smiling when you read what happened. At least I hope you were because that is the one and only point of all this.

And that was it, three boys, one undersized ball and bingo, success, a story for children that makes old men and women feel good. And one of the best things about children's stories is, you can go over them again and get the same result, even if you know what's going to happen. Even without reading, a four-year-old would understand the pictures and feel good.

Plus it is really easy to find and retell that story. All you need is a bench in a park near a basketball court, or tennis, or soccer, or anything. Just make sure an adult is around and you can help revive the tales of innocence.

10

The Impossible Game

Once again, all these stories are simple. They are the kind you could pick up walking through a park or driving down a street, like on Number 5 Road in Richmond near Steveston Highway.

But this, in some other countries, looks bad. A bunch of kids, grade six and seven, leaving a Muslim school and heading for the Jewish school down the street.

"We're going to beat them bad," said one boy who had Middle Eastern ancestry.

"We're going to whip them," said a girl with a head scarf.

There were a lot of them, maybe thirty or more. They looked determined.

Number 5 Road also has a Buddhist temple and places for Christians and Hindus. Some call it the Highway to Heaven.

On this day some kids were standing at the entrance to the Jewish school.

"Let them try. They think they're so good, but we'll beat them," said a boy with a skull cap.

The two groups stood face to face. In ninety percent of the rest of the world there would be blood shed in the next few minutes.

"Welcome," said the principal of the Jewish school.

"Thank you," said the principal of the Muslim school.

The Jews opened their ranks and the Muslims walked between them. There was a lot of nervous giggling.

A few minutes later both sides were on the basketball court.

The Jews had the ball. The Muslims had the ball. Jews. Muslims. Jews. Shoot. Miss. Muslims. Shoot. Miss.

On the sidelines the cheerleaders, who were all girls, cheered. One side had head scarves, the other didn't. Except for that and the names of the teams, the cheers were the same.

Ella Levy, principal of the Jewish school: "We just want to get together and have fun and see this as normal."

Zainab Dhanani, principal of the Muslim school: "We want to show our children this is not only possible, but actual."

"Who's going to win?" I asked.

Two women grinned. Each wanted to say their team, or at least I guessed they did. That's what I would say.

"The best team," they both said at once.

That is why they are principals. I had to leave before the game was over but I knew who won. We did.

11

A Tree for Alika

On East Broadway, near Fraser, a man named Frank used to live and do business. He is no longer in this world, but he did good while he visited here.

He had a junk business that spilled out his front door and onto the sidewalk.

"It is a poor neighbourhood," he said. "I sell things cheap, but I buy them even cheaper." He could have graduated from Harvard Business School.

His usual offerings were old tables and chairs and brooms and mops with a little life left in them. Sometimes there were television sets that would work if you got the rabbit ears just right. And the day I was there, a bird cage was for sale. No bird.

I stopped because I saw a dark-skinned woman with the semblance of some African dress standing at Frank's door negotiating the sale of a Christmas tree.

Frank did not sell Christmas trees. That would be big business and his was a small business. He did not charge tax. He did not pay tax. He did not care. He made a living and satisfied local needs and that was good enough, even if there was no line on his tax form that asked about local needs.

"He wants $20," said the woman who told me her name was Alika. "I will only pay $15."

"But it is a $25 tree," said Frank. "I paid almost that much for it."

Alika said she had come from East Africa and had been here

58

only a few years, but in that time her children had gotten to like Christmas. "They want to decorate a tree."

The tree looked like it had been a veteran of many Christmases past but it was still in one piece and could stand up to another set of lights and tinsel.

I asked her what she knew about Christmas and she said, "I know that it is when Jesus was born, but I am a Muslim and I believe something else."

"So why are you getting a tree?"

"For my children."

That was everything that Christmas is about.

"Was Jesus born under a tree?" she asked.

I did a double take. That was one of those insightful observations that I had never thought about. Of course she would think that. Any reasonable person would think that if they had not been taught to believe something different.

"No, he was born in a stable, a very poor family."

"Then why do you decorate trees?"

I wanted to explain about the Easter bunny and Santa Claus, and how they have nothing and yet everything to do with the big events of the Christian world, but there was no way I could begin when both she and Frank had their hands on the tree between them.

"Because it is nice and makes you feel good," I said.

"That's what I want for my kids."

In the end this Muslim mother went home with a Christmas tree wrapped in a garbage bag under her arm. "My kids will be happy. And I got it for $15," she whispered, triumphantly, to me.

"I let her have it for $15," said Frank. "You can call it my present to her."

And that was it for Frank's Christmas tree sales for the season, one tree that would make some kids and their mother happy. I could not explain the meaning of that to her, but luckily I would not have to.

12

The Strange Tale of the $100 Bill

This is a personal note and thank you to a woman who did a very nice thing.

A while ago I did a story on television about a man selling flowers by the side of the road. He had lung cancer, a raspy voice, no gloves and was living wherever he could find a spot to crawl into at night. His name, TJ. That's enough of a name when you haven't anything else.

Shortly after the story was on the air someone sent a cardboard box to me filled with scarves and sweaters and gloves. There was also a new $100 bill in a card that wished TJ good luck and said she would say a prayer for him. A separate note asked if I would give this to TJ. There was no return address, no signature and nothing that in any way would let me trace the person who had sent it. That made the gift even nicer. No credit was asked for.

I put the box in my trunk, but there is a problem with people who live outside the mainstream of life that most of the rest of us spend our days in. If you meet someone with a job or someone who is in school or who has a home it is fairly simple to find that person again. They will be at work or school or home, obviously. But not if you are homeless.

There's another problem, which I discussed with my wife and several people at work. What would he do with a $100 bill? Would someone grab it from him and say he stole it? Would he be able to spend it? Should I change it to $20s or $10s for his sake?

No. Someone had sent him this, and he would get this. Whatever the outcome, it was intended as a gift and it would be given that way. I had no right to interfere.

I drove back to the same street where I had met TJ, but it was empty. I circled a few blocks but no luck. I went home.

The next day, and every day for weeks, I looked for TJ. Sometimes there would be some flower petals on that corner, or a nearby corner, but no one selling them. I transferred the box to a camera van every morning, and several times a day during our cruising around the city looking for something new I would ask the cameramen to pass by that street, which was near GM Place. We never saw him.

A few times I wandered around skid row asking for him. I got some leads; he was here, he was there, no, they had never heard of him, yes, he's my friend, what's his name again?

Winter became spring and then summer and I had still not seen him. He might be in a rooming house, I was told, so I knocked on every door I could find. Every one of the few that opened had someone behind it who said he wasn't here.

Summer turned into fall and I felt so bad for TJ, who was missing out on something good, and for the woman who sent the gift. I had thought if I found TJ I would do a story about the gift so that she would know, and others would know that someone did something good. I knew it was a woman because of the way she wrote. Women are more gentle than men.

I also knew the box was not doing me or anyone any good and I thought if I didn't find him soon, maybe in another week or two, I would give it all to Union Gospel Mission.

Then one day I was driving home with my wife over the Georgia Viaduct and I glanced over the side and saw TJ on the corner, with his flowers. Whooh. Quick. Off at the Main Street exit and circle the block, and there he still was, with two of the most unsavoury people I would not wish anyone to be with.

You are allowed to jump to conclusions when you see someone with not just a lean and hungry look but also a mean and nasty look. There was a man and a woman and they did not appear to be nice. It was clear that they were together and TJ was the outsider. Also, my wife said she did not like that couple and if she says she does not like someone they are not likeable, period.

I walked over to all of them. Mr. Nasty and Mrs. Nasty looked suspicious. TJ looked happy to see me.

"Hi, how you doing?" The usual stuff. Then I told TJ that I had something for him and he should come with me. As soon as I said that I could see the attention perk up of Ugly Him and Nasty Her. Something for TJ would surely mean something, or possibly all of something, for them. But there was no other way of giving him a cardboard box without them noticing.

I introduced him to my wife, then opened my trunk and took out the box. I could see the other two measuring it from forty feet away. I opened it and said someone had sent these gloves and scarves for him and that he could share them, if he liked. I said they came from a woman who sent it, but I didn't know her name.

He did not hear much of anything I was saying. He was getting something, a present, and I suspect the last time that happened was when he was ten, maybe younger.

Then I slid the envelope out of the box and held it in front of him while his back was toward his friends.

"TJ, there is something else for you, but you cannot share it."

I opened the envelope with the card and the bill and he just stared. He didn't touch it, he just looked.

"For me?"

"Yes, from a nice lady."

"I've never seen one of those. For me?"

"Yes, but you can't tell your friends. Not at all, nothing. You can't hint at it, you can't let them know anything. You understand. This is not for them. It is for you."

He was still looking at the bill.

"Can I touch it?"

"Of course. It's yours. But fold it up and put it in your pocket and tell no one."

He did, but he did not want to take his hand out of his pocket.

"Here," I said, putting the box in his arms. "Share these."

Then he walked away.

"I hope he doesn't tell about the money," my wife said to me.

"Me too. They look like shysters who could smell money."

For the next year I did not see TJ again. Then one morning I got a call from Clive Jackson, the assignment editor at Global.

"I have bad news for you. Remember your friend with the flowers? Someone killed him."

No, I thought. That hurts. How do you know?

A fellow was found dead in a back alley near Yale Town. He had flowers in his hand and on his body. Video surveillance cameras had seen a car speeding through the alley, then it stopped and two men walked hurriedly back, then left.

The cameras did not see what happened, but it was clear that some idiots racing through the lane had hit him, then kept going. They came back to see his condition, and whether he was alive or not no one will ever know. He was dead by the time someone found him. Like most who live on the streets he had no identification.

But the police in Vancouver are very good. They knew about TJ and his flowers and they knew that I knew him. John Daly, who is the best police reporter I have ever known, knew about the death and got a copy of the story from the office and the police used it to identify the victim of the murder, or the accident, whichever it was.

I went to the alley. The cops were there. It was not TJ. He is not the only one selling flowers. Someone else who was selling flowers had been hit by a car going fast through a back alley. The driver and his passenger came back to check. The man with the flowers was dead. If they got away quickly enough no one would ever know. And so far, no one does.

It is not the way police dramas end on television.

Later that same night—and here is where the unexplained ironies of life come in—my wife and I were downtown coming out of a movie.

"What to buy a tulip?"

"Hey, it's you. TJ."

"Yes, and it's you."

Unbelievable to be seeing him now. "How are you?" I asked.

"You would not believe it," he said. "I live in social housing, right on Granville Street. It is clean and neat. And I feel good."

"What happened with the $100?"

"Well, I kept it for a long time. I didn't know if I could spend it. But everything happened good after that. I got into social housing and I sold a lot more flowers. And I still had the $100."

"Did you ever spend it?"

He looked sheepish. "Yes, I bought some clothes and a couple of good meals. And now everything is going good. I hated to get rid of it but I am doing well."

"You buy any beer or anything?" I asked, trying to see if he had done with the money what some might think he would have done.

"No. I don't drink." Then he added, "It was nice of the lady to give it to me."

"What happened with the people who were with you when I gave you the money?" I asked.

"They didn't believe I only got the box. They kept asking if I got anything else. We got into a fight. Then they took the box and left."

I gave him five dollars for one tulip and gave the flower to my wife. TJ and I shook hands, then he shook hands with my wife and he disappeared into the crowd. He had to go back to work.

Whoever you are who sent the money, you did well. If you are ever downtown and see TJ selling flowers and you tell him who you are I'm sure he will give you a bouquet, for free. I am also sure you would never tell him. Thank you.

13

The Listener

I always thought my friend Billy was brilliant. He taught me to do things differently, like Rule Two. He taught me to do things differently from the way most expect them to be done.

In television and movies continuity is an iron-hard rule. If a hat is on a man in one scene it must be on his head in the next. But in real life the hat could have been knocked off when you were not looking. In reality, things don't go smoothly. If you do things the way others expect you to do them you will escape scorn. But you might not discover amazing quirks.

We grew up in the city, the real inner-inner-city part of New York, with no birds except pigeons and people said they were really just rats with wings. But for fun we had a highway near us, the Van Wick Expressway. If you have landed at JFK airport you probably took a taxi on that roadway getting to the tall buildings of Manhattan. We lived in a different part of New York. We were surrounded by factories and railroads. It was the gall bladder part of the city. You would not visit there, but that's the part of the city that helps keep the rest of the city alive.

When you passed the Atlantic Avenue exit on your way to Manhattan you went under what we called one of the seven wonders of the world, or at least our world. There were, still are, five train trestles that go over the highway at that spot. That was our playground. We would climb up under the steel girders and watch the trains going over our heads and the cars down below our feet.

If you are a parent, never ask your kids what they really did during the afternoon. If they look happy, and alive, you can be happy.

We developed a game called Name the Truck. There were lots of trucks going out to the airport and we would try to be the first to spot them: Kenworth! Wrong. Mac! Bummer.

But one kid up there, Billy, was almost always right. "Freightliner." "Yup." "Peterbilt." "Right again." And he would call out their names often before we could see them.

"How do you do this magic trick?" we asked.

"Secret," he said. "I have trucks in my veins."

We had no idea what having anything in your veins meant but the adults always said that, so we had everything in our veins: trucks, comic books, baseball and, as we got older, love. Then one day he whispered his secret to me. "I listen for them. That's all. They each sound different."

I had never thought of that and it was so obvious. He had seen something that we all saw, but he saw it differently. That was one of the great lessons in life. If you think or look at something from somewhere different, you get a different view.

After that I tried to walk a different route to school each day and found streets I did not know existed. That way of dealing with things is not in any textbooks but it is simple and fascinating. The rest of my life has been pretty much the same.

"I want you to do a story on the murderer."

This was in the old days of crime reporting when there were many murders.

"How about we do something about the victim instead?"

"I don't care what you do, just make it good."

"With the victim, it will be good."

Fifty years after listening to the trucks on the highway I was looking for something to brighten my day as always, and to share on television if I could. I was with cameraman Roger Hope and we saw a woman with binoculars looking for birds in a park at the edge of the city.

That's good enough for me. The starting position for any story is anywhere that someone is breathing. Looking for birds is a bonus.

She said she was with her husband and he was the real bird watcher. "He knows everything about them," and we should talk to him, but he was lagging behind, looking at a bird. "I'll have to shout to get him here. He doesn't hear very well."

Poor guy, I thought.

Her name, Rosemary, his, Dave, and they have been birding together forty-five years since they met. Before they were a couple he was a birder, she wasn't.

"She had to become interested if she wanted to stay interested in me," he laughed.

This is also Rule Four, good people make good stories, no matter what.

I interviewed them both for quite a while, trying to find something quirky about bird watching. They were friendly, but they kept talking about birds, imagine that.

They spoke of the beauty and tenacity and the flight paths, but said nothing that was different, until Rosemary mentioned "often you can hear them before you see them."

Suddenly, bingo. It was like the nerve endings in my head said, "Whooh, did she say 'hear them?' She has a hobby of seeing and she mentions hearing." Zoom, a Freightliner went ripping by below my feet. "See, I was right," said Billy.

I stopped asking questions. The cameraman slid over close to me and said he guessed we better be going because there was nothing he heard that was different.

"Just wait, and please, just tape them while they look for birds," I asked. Poor cameraman Roger, he had never met Billy.

He shot beautiful pictures of Rosemary and David walking on the edge of a bank of trees, she pointing at something in a tree and then both of them raising their binoculars. We stayed back as far as possible and saw repeatedly she would point and he would look.

I could only hear traffic on a street nearby and the beep of a truck backing up and a chainsaw. We approached Rosemary and David again and I asked and she said, "If you concentrate you can hear the birds. Each chirp is different."

David said he had lost all his high-range hearing. He had worked around loud machinery before anyone put noise and hearing loss together. Sometimes the simple math of life escapes us all.

"I can't hear the winter wren any longer," said David. "That makes me sad."

The words coming from behind his white beard and lined face were more than sad—they were tragic.

"So I listen," said Rosemary, "and he looks and he tells me what we are seeing."

They went off together, at the edge of the trees, pointing and looking and walking and loving. Forty-five years together, she now helping him with what he taught her.

For them, everything worked.

14

Birds for Life

Again, as on almost every day of my life, I was on the hunt. I would like to find something that is funny or touching or meaningful. Actually, anything with a twist or a moral or a smile, anything, so long as it is something. I like to keep the parameters broad.

Then I saw another bird watcher. He made a beautiful sight because mist was rising off Beaver Lake in Stanley Park and it was travelling up on sunbeams that were squeezing between the leaves of trees. I like to find things that look good and surely anything this pretty must have substance as well as beauty.

We spoke. His name, Stan Piontek, and he was looking for a diver. He had not seen one yet today.

He made an imitation of its song and showed how it swooped while it was flying. This man likes his divers, I thought.

The usual question: "Come here often?"

The answer that made me love him: "Every day."

Of course he could have said this was his first day and that would be as good, or he could have said he comes here frequently, or seldom, or never again. Every answer has its own magic. But every day is best.

"For how long?"

"Long," he said.

I felt guilty because he did not really want to talk now. He was pleasant to us, but he was looking for a diver and you can't do that and talk to nosy strangers.

"How long, if you don't mind me asking." I know I am a terrible intruder and a pain, but honestly, he said "Long" and I wanted to know how long, but at the same time I did not want to make him say "Too long now that you are here."

Being inquisitive is a delicate balance. It is like most human conditions—"Please give me more, just a little more, I don't want to take too much, but more, please."

That fits the need with cookies, cartoons and, as we grow older, with sex. "Just one more question/cookie/kiss." And then we learn the great human quandary: more is never enough. I believe we descended from sponges.

"I've come here every day for forty-five years," he said.

"Do you mean every day?"

"Yes, it is always new."

He really said that.

"Every day?"

I really said that. I missed the importance of what he said for the sensationalizing of what I heard.

"Yes, every day. Oh, I've missed a few, but every day for 45 years. The same year as hurricane Hazel. That was 1955."

And if you do the math, that was more than ten years ago that I met him, and I still remember the sight of this solitary human walking through sunbeams looking for a particular bird. All it takes is a sunbeam to remind me.

"I came here before they finished the seawall. It was only up to Second or Third Beach when I first found this spot. There were deer tracks then and no wide trails like now."

I was thinking the seawall had been there forever. No one I had met before Stan could talk about a time before the seawall.

He was another of those travellers through time and space.

"But it's always new and fascinating," he said. "And today, like I said, I'm looking for a diver."

Why? And what do divers do?

"They go into water falls and disappear, then they come out again."

"No waterfalls here."

"That's why it's hard to find them, but I will."

Stan told me he had no family and he lived in a one-room apartment in the West End. He had lived there forever and for the same length of time he had come here. He brought a small pair of binoculars, almost like opera glasses, not big and powerful with wide angle lenses like I have seen with other bird watchers.

"These are fine," he said. "I've had them for a long time."

He showed us some other birds. They were easy to spot. But no divers.

"I enjoy this. That's all. You get so used to coming here you just keep on coming and keep on enjoying it."

We stayed with him for another quarter of an hour while he patiently hunted for what he wanted to see. I could only guess his age—in his 70s, maybe 80s—but he looked healthy, which must have been a gift of the daily outings.

"That's enough for today," he said. He said goodbye to us and then walked off through the sunbeams, almost like a dream, except he was real and the sunbeams were real and this fascinating place was real. It was all he needed and all he wanted. Unlike me with my questioning, he did not want any more.

He turned one time to wave to us, and then I realized why it was not a disappointing thing that he did not find a diver. He had a reason to come back tomorrow.

15

History By One Who Was There

Aweek before Christmas in 2006 one of the biggest wind storms ever in the history of the entire universe, more or less, came off the gulf and kicked and hammered the western chin of Stanley Park. It was a nasty assault without warning in the night, sort of a sucker punch. Something like this had only happened a few times before and the attacks came from typhoons, so you kind of expect them even if you don't like them.

But on the night of December 16, the wind came and then came again and again like a gang of hoodlums, beating up the park, hitting it until it was down and then kicking it more. When it ended, to mix a metaphor, the park in many places was toothless. Ten thousand trees were killed.

The pictures on television could not give you the immensity of it. They were like pictures of war. They are informative, but it's not like being there. Those who went after the roads were cleared enough to get through drove slowly, staring, turning their heads, saying nothing. It was devastation in every direction.

Among the trees was one that had been cut in half by park workers so it could be bulldozed off the road. It was a cedar, and lying on its side it came up to my shoulders. I felt tiny.

One of the park's arborists said she estimated the tree to be about five or six hundred years old. It was impossible to count the rings since the central core of a cedar rots while the outside stays strong and grows. Only cedars know why cedars do this.

But we could start counting from the outside in. The rings were tight, ten fitting under the width of my pinkie finger. The woods were thick and growth was slow.

I made a mark with a felt pen at about sixty years earlier: World War II; the tree was a giant while cannons a short walk away in the park were aimed at the sea waiting for an invasion. Another mark about a hundred years in the past: World War I, and a soldier was taking his last trip through the park with his special girl before going off to the trenches in Europe where he would be gassed and spend the rest of his life barely able to breath.

Another mark about 150 years ago. The counting is difficult because the rings are so close together, but this is a rough history seen over rough lines: 1858 and the gold seekers are landing by the tens of thousands along the Fraser River. They don't walk past this tree, they are rushing up the river looking for the lottery in the ground.

But along with them come others who saw the trees, giant trees, and saw gold under the bark. "You might or you might not find yellow metal, but there is a forest of wealth right in front of us."

So they started to collect it. The rich ones hired men to cut by hand, to use axes on trees that were six or seven hundred years old. Because the centres of the trees were rotten, the orders were to cut the trees from about ten feet off the ground.

So these poor men had to cut notches in the trees, then insert wooden planks that they called springboards, then climb on the boards and hack away at the trees. When you think of beautiful giants going down it is sad. When you think of the men who had to cut them, that is also sad. It is hard enough to stand on the ground and swing a two-headed axe. It is nearly impossible to do it while keeping your balance on a board eighteen inches wide, ten feet off the ground.

But they cut and sawed and the giants fell by the hundreds of thousands, maybe millions, and were then dragged out of the woods by oxen who also did not have overly good lives. The logs were pulled over trails made of other logs placed horizontally across the road and covered with grease—hence skid road.

The old skid roads then became the ways into the woods for people who lived in shacks, who could not afford city life. Later beer parlours and cheap hotels grew up along the skid roads and the largest of them in this rapidly disappearing part of the forest later became the 100 block of East Hastings.

Anyway, our lovely dead cedar was probably just too small in the 1800s to bother cutting when five separate logging companies were working in the forests that became the park. The remains of our tree's older cousins are still there, stumps with springboard holes in them.

Our tree was lucky.

I made another mark about three hundred years ago when the tree was the size of a fat telephone pole. Somewhere under that mark Wolfgang Amadeus Mozart performed before the Imperial Court in Vienna. The tree was still alive when a movie was made about Mozart's life three centuries later.

"This is about fifty years ago, when we came to Canada," a couple said. They had a Dutch accent and were pointing to rings not far from the bark.

That was what was important to them, of course. Our own lives trump Mozart's any day and when you see a way of looking back and making a connection you have stepped through time and space, and that of course is impossible, unless you do it.

The tree knew nothing of our histories. This exercise in counting rings was just us putting our histories into something else.

The only strange thing to me was not that the tree was so old, but that I had never noticed it before it was killed. It was just one more mammoth in a thick, old forest of mammoths.

It was like going to a funeral and hearing wonderful things about someone and thinking, "I should have spent more time visiting and listening."

I could have looked at that tree while it was standing and been amazed that it was in that same spot when the greatest art explosion of all time was happening in Italy: Leonardo da Vinci was painting the *Mona Lisa*, Michelangelo was hacking *David* out of a hunk of stone and painting the ceiling of the Sistine Chapel.

The tree was just a sapling then.

And it was alive when Martin Luther hammered his complaints about the abuses of the Church on the door of a church. Luther got into deep doo-doo for that, but he started one of the greatest anti-old-religion, pro-new-religion movements in the history of the world.

The tree was spreading out its tender branches.

And it was alive when Machiavelli wrote a book called *The Prince*, which was the first how-to book on making a successfully corrupt government. His work seems to be universally followed now. If you haven't read it, try it. You will say, "Those bums, that's what they are doing to me now."

The tree was only as tall as you and I then, but it was breathing and growing, which were its main duties.

And it was alive when Henry VIII said, "Up yours" to the

Pope, which was not a sanctioned thing to do, and started a new church, which many Canadians belong to. Henry was driven to this action because he was like many film stars and golf pros of today. They wanted what the Pope said no-no to. You want how many wives? Henry just happened to be a king so he could get away with it.

The tree was growing and feeling the breezes off the Pacific waters when Jacques Cartier sailed up the St. Lawrence River. That is why you have French labels on your English HP sauce today.

That same tree lived through all this, then was killed by a mugger in the night. The irony of that alone is worth a shake of the head, and worth a visit to a park to stand in awe beneath some ancient beings. It would also be good to visit some old friend and ask before it is too late: "Tell me about your childhood."

16

The Fridge Magnet Car

Another children's book, just waiting to be taken off the shelf. All I needed was the librarian to check it out.

It was in the parking lot of Trout Lake, where I met Reilly the autistic nine-year-old who taught me everything is possible. So I knew this would work.

I was almost giddy. Okay, it was not almost. I *was* giddy, looking at a 1989 Chevy, sort of rust red with a few strokes of real rust and a couple of dents and, most importantly of all, half covered with fridge magnets. This you don't see every day. Yes, some days you see a lot of decals on cars. And some days you see an Art Car, carefully created by artistic people who put everything on their cars, like water fountains and rocket ships. Those I have looked at and marvelled and jumped, a tiny bit, and done stories about. Art Cars and decals belong to species of humans who are making a statement. I like statements. They say something, even if I don't know what it is.

But refrigerator magnets are entirely different. Everyone has magnets on their refrigerators. As postcards go out of style (because who actually could wait a week or two to get holiday pictures delivered?), fridge magnets are IN. Every tourist shop in the world sells them. And every tourist buys them.

"Here's the pyramids. I bought that right next to one of the real pyramids. It's got a strong magnet. It can hold a month of lottery tickets under it. I've got to check those someday."

The fridge has become the photo album, with kids and grand-kids and friends all held on by magnets of alligators from the Everglades and Guinness Beer from St. James's Gate. That's where Guinness was born and where you get a free glass of the stout at the end of the tour of the historic brewery, which is still leased at the equivalent of $100 a year for 9,000 years because the original owners thought it was a joke that anyone would make such a bot-tom level, bitter beer and make any money at it.

"I'll take lemonade," said my wife.

"What!!! This is Guinness from where Guinness is made in Ireland," said I with eyebrows that were scraping the Irish sky.

"I don't like beer," she said.

So she had lemonade, in the brewery where Guinness comes from. I think that is a sin. We came home with fridge magnets from Guinness at St. James's Gate, but I still think of that lemon-ade, which means I left with two memories—the Guinness I had and the Guinness I did not have.

Anyway, here in Trout Lake there were fridge magnets on the car in the parking lot. Not everyone has stickers, outside of *The Fox Rocks* and *Go, Canucks Go*, and not everyone is an artist who can turn a car into a moving studio. But everyone has magnets, so this was a car for everyone.

I went into the rec centre knowing I was looking for, who?

On the skating rink I picked trendy people. "Do you have magnets on your car?"

Weird question. "No."

In the gym where badminton was being played. "Fridge magnets?"

"Please, we're playing, and no."

I went out to the parking lot to wait. The car was gone. Gone? How? Please don't tell me it is gone. I was inside only a few minutes. Darn, and worse words.

For the next six months I checked the parking lot a couple of times a week. Nothing, so we went on with our lives and found other items of interest.

"Someday I will find the magnets," I said believing that I would someday find the magnets.

Then one day the car was there again in the parking lot, with the driver just about ready to leave. "Hello." "Hello, and yes, that's my car."

But this time I am on my own. I wander the city sometimes looking for interesting things when I have no cameraman with me. The desperate call: "I have fridge magnets. I found them. Send someone."

In the office I know what they are saying and I am lucky I cannot hear them.

"He has fridge magnets. He would like us maybe to call the guys off the murder to look at magnets. Or maybe he would like us to call someone in on overtime to see something stuck to something."

Lucky I was not there. I had also not spoken another word to the woman who owned the magnets and the car to which they were attached.

"I have to go," she said.

I call back to the office. "Fridge magnets will un-stick soon. Please. Hurry."

Hollywood seldom reaches excitement like this. And I know you would do the same thing if you suddenly found the magnets you had been searching for and there was a threat that they might go away before you could get your story to tell at dinner. Things like this take on great importance. Everything is important at the time it is important—that's the human spice that we add to life.

I have to give credit to someone special. You never hear his name or see his face, but he is one of the reasons I have stayed at Global past retirement. He is the person who dispatches cameras, Doug Sydora. It is beyond difficult—no, it is beyond impossible—to get cameramen to all the events that need recording and all the events that producers think need recording.

There are always more events than cameras. In the past, before Doug arrived at the station, I would wait until two or three p.m. for a camera. The last story on the show was not the top priority. At three p.m. I was dying, wondering how on earth or heaven I would ever get my work done.

When Doug came from a smaller television station in Alberta he found a way to reorganize the same numbers and get me going, usually before the early bird had even picked out a worm.

"Start now? This early? I'm not awake."

"Get going," he would say. "Some other reporters are still waiting for inspiration."

I don't know how he did it, but with a cameraman I could hunt for a story. With a story I could continue working. Without Doug, whom you will never see on TV, I would not be there now. That is another management course. Give people what they need and they will give you the same.

My phone rang. "Ten minutes away and we hope that magnets are more important than a life and death press conference."

"When would they not be?" I said, believing that press conferences should be banned from the news. They are a funnelling of information. You should get the information and then apply it to the story, not make it the story. Besides, officials talking are rarely telling you anything except official-speak, which is not translatable.

"I have to get to my next appointment," said magnet lady.

"Please, just a few minutes."

Her name was Kaye Atkinson and she taught classes in stroke recovery. That is very nice. That is also why I kept missing her. Her classes were in the mornings and I usually got there about noon. Today was a wonderful fluke.

"Why do you have these on your car?"

That was the clincher of the question. That was the reason why this would entertain and enlighten half a million people in a few hours. I just did not know what that reason was. Imagine, fridge magnets on her car because… "No real reason," she said.

What??? There must be something. You can't do something for nothing. Okay, you can, but not today, not now, not when they have taken the camera away from the life and death press conference.

"But why?" That was me, pleading again.

"I just had some extra magnets and I thought my father would think it's funny."

Ahhh, something. You just never can give up on anything, including magnets.

"Why?"

"Well, he died and left me his car and he would never, ever, do anything like this," Kaye said. "So the first magnet I got was B-B-Q Champ. He loved barbecuing. This is in homage to him."

The camera arrived. No questions asked. This was better than being inside a room with other photographers all taking pictures of someone's head with words coming out of the mouth. You take one picture, without moving.

But here: close-ups, wide angles, pans, zooms, the works. Fridge magnets as art, as a statement, as you have never seen them before. Fridge magnets to make someone who has been transferred to the great attraction in the sky smile when he looks down at his old car.

"Asparagus, why asparagus?"

"Because it was there."

"The Chop and Wok. Do you eat at the Chop and Wok?"

"Never been there. I just ended up with their magnet."

She started right after her father died and it made her smile. That was the sum total extent of it. They made one woman feel good because she thought it would make someone else feel good, even if he wasn't here. Nice people do make good stories, even if the story is not earth shaking. In fact, there is no need to shake the earth. It just felt good for a moment.

Two hundred magnets and room for more. Some were stolen from the fenders and doors, or got blown off in the wind, so she now glues them on. It will be hard to sell her car, but then Kaye does not intend to do that. She drives what her father drove and it makes her glad.

As she drove off to help the next rehab class the last magnet I saw was "You Go Girl."

Yes, she did.

17

Flowers in the Hubcap

You can look at this as a children's story or a business textbook.

In the children's version a poor immigrant from China who struggled with English did the only thing he knew he could do. He opened his own small auto fix-it shop. His name was Poon and he called his shop Poon's Auto Repair Shop.

His shop was on a street in a poor area with not many people living nearby who had cars.

Poon worked very hard, with his wife helping him. She stood behind the counter selling batteries and oil and keeping the books.

Soon they had a little girl named Alice who grew up in the shop. She played with old tires and tools and helped out as best she could.

"It is very tiring work," said Poon, "but I will not take a day off because we need all the pennies we can get."

"I wish something good would happen to us," said his wife, "so that our child does not have to grow up with the smell of greasy rags and the sight of broken motors all around her. I wish she could have flowers to play with." She told me she used to say that.

And then one day something did happen. A bulldozer moved onto the empty space across the street and began clearing the land. And then construction crews came and put up a large building with an even larger parking lot.

"I wonder if it will be a happy place, maybe a restaurant or a clothing store," said Mrs. Poon. "Maybe the customers will see us and bring their cars to us." But they knew that would probably not happen since most people use auto repair shops close to their homes for the sake of convenience.

Then the sign went up on the building.

"It is not a happy place," said Mrs. Poon. The sign said Glenhaven Funeral Home.

"They will not be thinking of having their cars fixed," said Poon.

"They will be very sad," said Mrs. Poon.

Alice looked past the piles of tires that were outside her front door and said, "But there is something people going to funerals need."

Her mother and father did not understand. They did not need tires or headlights or oil, and if they did they would not be buying them while they were dressed in their best clothing.

In the next picture in the children's book or the next chapter in the business text was Alice who was standing by a broken engine. "They need flowers," she said.

"But we have no flowers here," said her father.

"Just you wait," said Alice.

She got her mother and herself signed up for a flower arranging class, then they got up very early in the morning and went to the flower auctions that are held at five a.m. every day inside big buildings on Marine Drive near Boundary Road in Burnaby.

"It is so beautiful in here," said Mrs. Poon. "And it smells so nice."

Rows of flower buyers sat in the clean and quiet auction room while cart after cart of roses and tulips and carnations were rolled in front of them. The buyers were from corner stores and super-markets and florists all over the city.

They knew what they wanted and they would have their flow-ers bought and be back on the road before most people in the city were awake. The flower business is not for those who sleep late.

Mrs. Poon and Alice bought all the flowers they thought they would need, then drove back to the auto fix-it shop. The first thing they did was get busy making wreaths and bouquets. Then they cleaned the grease off the front window and swept the entrance way.

They put the flowers on display next to the tires and along their security fence and on the counter where spark plugs were no longer stored. Then they put up a sign that said, "Funeral Flowers."

Anyone parking their car across the street would see the sign.

"That's a strange place to buy flowers," said a man in a black suit who had just parked.

"But we should have flowers before we go in," said his wife.

The first flowers were sold before the first funeral had begun.

It is an odd sight, old tires next to new flowers. You can see it on East Hastings at Salisbury Drive. Behind the window where the office used to be is now a florist shop with Mrs. Poon and Alice working in it. Three steps away through a swinging door is a car on a hoist with Mr. Poon working below it.

"It smells much better in here now, and it is also happy and cheerful," said Alice.

The last picture shows a world of grease next door to a world of colour with Alice surrounded by flowers.

In the children's book it is a happy ending. In the business textbook it is the same.

18

One More Tin Soldier

Allstories become memories. You don't have to store them or organize them or dust them off. They just stay somewhere in your head, basically ignored, no watering or wrapping required, until unexpectedly, five or fifty years later, you hear or see or smell something and pop, out comes the story.

"Hey, that reminds me of this guy, this woman, this dog, this thing, and you know what happened???"

Stories are their own form of gold, except you can share them and keep them, unlike the hard stuff.

The old cannon in Port Moody suddenly reminded me of the tiny old cannons I saw in a home twenty years earlier. For two decades the story had sat untouched, and then suddenly I had to tell everyone.

I had heard about a man named Joe Woosnam who made tin soldiers. Many people, or at least it used to be many before computer war games, had a hobby of collecting tin soldiers. Girls had dolls and guys had tin soldiers because in the dusty past of humankind we found a way of leaving women behind with babies while the men went to war almost constantly, at least since the doors of the Garden of Eden closed on us.

And when you have an army you have to have a uniform for your soldiers, otherwise how would anyone know they were your soldiers and not the other guy's? Without a uniform who would you shoot at? If you came marching over a hill without everyone in a uniform you might look like just a bunch of farmers going to chase crows and who would be afraid of that?

So uniforms were ordered and the soldiers got dressed before going off defending or invading, but that was not good enough. As every fashion conscious invader or defender knows, you have to have the best-looking uniform, certainly better than those you are intent on blowing apart.

Over centuries, every country, every state, every king and queen, every army and navy down to every division within every army and navy had to look different, and better, than every other one. There were sashes and hats and feathers and breast plates and jackets and boots and stripes on the trousers and kilts and cuffs, and if you have ever been in the military you know your cuffs had to be exactly right or you would have to do push-ups

War without distinctive style leads to guerrilla warfare without uniforms. "Whose side are you on? You have a red bandana and I have a green bandana. Should we shoot each other?"

That well-known war stylist Che Guevara came along briefly and changed the guerrilla look forever. You could not be a radical unless you had a floppy beret and an uncombed beard and a tee-shirt with a picture of Che and his floppy beret and uncombed beard.

"You have a beret, I have a beret. Let's shoot someone else."

This all led to Joe, who had been in the army during World War II and worked in an office after that and then one day saw one tin soldier in a hobby shop window.

"It was beautiful. It had so many colours," he said.

He bought it and immediately wanted more, which is what keeps all hobby shops alive. But Joe was an inventive guy. Why should he buy more when he could make his own army? Occasionally he would find on the streets small lead weights that are used to balance car tires. The wheels turn smoothly until the weights fall off. You know the car ahead of you is missing its wheel weights when one of the tires is like a high-speed drummer doing a solo at 80 clicks an hour. Bad for the tires, good for Joe.

He collected the weights, made a hard, heatproof mould shaped from the soldier he bought, melted the lead weights in a tiny pot and then poured the thick, hot liquid metal into the mould.

Presto, his first recruit. He made many more. He made every army and navy he could research. He had shelf after shelf of them. Each one in the exact, true colours and style of their time, but there were more to make, always more. That is the beauty of a hobby—if you are true to it you can never finish it.

He bought some of the soldiers to use as starting points but he also carved some of them out of plasticine and then hunted for lost weights. All this despite being blind in one eye.

It was the fact that his hobby cost him almost nothing that appealed to some. But what I liked best was one comment that went something like: "Sometimes I worked until two or three o'clock in the morning trying to get the paint right, then get three or four hours sleep, go to work, and then rush home to finish it."

That's what keeps us alive.

And then I asked how many he had made, because his basement room with shelves everywhere had at least ten thousand soldiers.

"This is what I display," he said. "I've made about three hundred thousand of them."

"Say that again, slowly."

"Yes, three hundred thousand. Some are in Europe, some across Canada and some in the States. I've given most of them away."

He began his hobby when he was fifty years old. He was eighty-two when I met him. He had the enthusiasm of someone who was just finishing boot camp.

There used to be a slogan that wars are not good for children and other living things. But uniforms can be mesmerizing, especially on soldiers and sailors and airmen who were recruited from the gutter and were turned into troops strong and stunning enough to fight off ugliness and boredom. General Joe won every battle and never fired a shot.

It was the sight of the old cannon in Port Moody that reminded me of old Joe.

19

Black Powder and Old Vets

They lit the black powder fuse. It sizzled in the rain but nothing happened. The camera was rolling but no bang was getting recorded.

They lit it again. Same thing—sizzle, poof, a little white smoke. No bang.

There was quiet in the crowd, and impatience and expectation and disappointment. I felt the same. If this had been a government sponsored event I knew I would be showing the failures, because when an official body fails it makes the unofficial world feel a little better.

But these were volunteer guys who were trying to add some power and fire and feeling to truly the most sacred day of the year. It was November 11, 2009, in Port Moody. Maybe half the people in Port Moody had come down to Clarke Street, next to the railroad tracks, to applaud the old soldiers and listen to the bands and see and feel the explosion of the old cannon.

No one in the crowd moaned. No one said, "Ah shucks." They waited, quietly.

An hour earlier the old cannon with its large wooden wheels had been taken off the back of a pickup truck. That was a strange sight. When cannons like this were used for killing they were dragged everywhere, usually by horses that would also often die in the struggle. Then the cannons were dragged by the shattered men who were left. War is hard.

"It is not really a cannon that was used anywhere in Canada," said one of the members of the Seymour Artillery Company, who was struggling to lower it from the truck. "But it will give an idea of old-time war."

That was for sure, because the next time they lit the fuse after drying the cannon and reloading it with black powder, it fired, it roared, it shouted and banged. It blasted out a dragon's tongue of flame and smoke and the crowd, and I, jumped.

"That was only half the powder they used to use," said the Artillery Sergeant.

A few car alarms went off, something else out of time and place.

"Don't worry, sweetheart, it's only noise," a father said to his terrified little girl who was crying and holding her ears. "We'll move back farther."

It is the duty of parents to protect their children.

The Seymour Artillery Company is the name of real life tin soldiers, with heart and pride. They re-enact armies of old. Their cannon, they said, was actually the type used in the US Civil War, but it was all they could get. Their uniforms were from a bygone age of pith helmets and red jackets. Their spirits were of every war in which every soldier has fought and been terrified.

It is the duty of a soldier to protect, even by killing.

In front of the Legion on Clarke Street, Sergeant Major Leo called his troops into line. At his age, he said, the first name would be enough. He shouted commands and eight men fell in, two in civilian clothes.

"Where's Jim?" someone asked.

"He's coming, I hope," someone answered.

We talked to some of the kids sitting on the wet curb. "I like the bands," said a girl. "I like the cannon," said a boy. Always it is that way.

The cameraman, John McCarron, nudged me and pointed to the window of the Legion that looked out over the marching old men. Inside, looking out, was one man in his uniform beret. "He would be our man," said John. John knows what makes something special. It is the one thing that is missing.

We went into the Legion and spoke to the man in the window. Jim was his name. When you are very young and very old one name seems to be all you need. You know who you are and labels are less important.

"My legs can't take it anymore," he said. "I want to be out there, but I just can't."

I know what he said was true because I could see, and John could see, the tear that was working its way out of one of his eyes. He wanted to be out there.

"I can't believe there's so few. I can't believe so many of my old buddies are gone."

He looked away from the window and asked us what we would like to know.

"Thank you," I said. "We have everything we would like to know."

It is the duty of children to grow strong and learn about wars.

It is the duty of their parents to prevent wars.

It is the duty of soldiers to win them.

It is the duty of old veterans to watch, and wonder, and remember.

20

It Also Rained in the Trenches

I t was raining. For the thirtieth year in a row I was at the Remembrance Day ceremony. I had no idea what to do.

In the past I have talked to old veterans whose stories can make your stomach tighten and your eyes water.

But it was raining and there was grumbling about the rain from some young people who had come to see the ceremony.

It was good that they came, but they were saying to each other that they were getting wet and they hoped they could get home quickly.

In the front rows were the veterans. It was raining on them.

I stood at the back of the wall of black umbrellas and wrote these words:

Nov. 11, 2008

Lest we forget, it also rained in the trenches. And it rained in the foxholes.

The mud in the trenches was over their knees. They could not move their feet. They could not walk. They could not sit down. If they did the mud came up to their chests. They could not lie down. They would drown.

They tried to sleep standing up, leaning against the walls of mud with the rain dripping off their helmets.

By November of the first year their rainproof ponchos were destroyed and the rain soaked through their woollen coats, and through their shirts, and through their skin.

When they were told to attack they slipped on the mud trying to climb out of the trenches. They slipped on the mud trying to run across no man's land. They slipped on the mud and fell onto the barbed wire. Their blood mingled with the mud.

The rain fell on the buildings in the next war. When the bombs exploded and the roofs were blown off, the rain fell on the dead inside.

In World War II it was raining in London when Edward R. Murrow reported over the radio that, "the fires reflecting on the wet glass made the windows look like they were crying tears of blood."

It rained on the children whose mothers and fathers and brothers and sisters were killed.

It rained on the endless columns of drenched soldiers marching across Europe. They did not have umbrellas or Gortex or rubber boots or Helly Hansen or North Face. They had only shivers, which went deep into their bones.

And then they were told to fight.

When today's ceremony ends we will all go home where it is dry.

They stayed, in the rain, so that we could go home.

21

Happy She, Sad She

Later I will tell you why I never use any camera trickery like slow motion or reversal of shots or…actually I don't know what else can be done since I never use it. That is, no slow-mo gets into a story without my saying we will now look at this in slow motion, just so you know and don't feel like the camera tricked you.

And then I met Dora and her friend, whose name I never got. They were walking together along the Fraser River in Coquitlam, near the Mary Hill Bypass. If you have never taken that walk, try it. In so many ways it looks like it did to the gold miners in 1858, except you have a gravel path, which is very nice.

We saw them coming toward us on a wet day and they were chatting, so we stopped them and asked one of the oldest questions: "Do you come here often?"

"Every day, every single day for years."

They both said it, one with a bit of annoyance, the other with pleasantness.

"You are friends."

"Yes, but Dora has a problem. She sees everything as nice and she is wrong and I am trying to convince her that things are not always good. And I watch your stories and you are like her, trying to make things good when they are not."

That was a big handful for a first answer.

Then Dora spoke. "She is so negative, but I try to show her the good things like the eagles along the river and the vegetation."

"You are so wrong, Dora. This area is getting overdeveloped and it will not be good for the next generation."

"But look how beautiful it is now, and you can see that and feel good."

"I prefer reality," said Dora's friend. "You are just like him," she said, pointing to me. "You pretend things are good when they are not. You are not living in the real world."

I was looking at two women who walk together for about an hour every day, "for years," and could not agree on the weather, much less the future of the world.

"How come you walk together?" I asked.

"I am trying to get her out of her negative viewpoint," said Dora.

"And I am trying to teach her how the world really is," said her friend without a name.

I usually ask everyone's names, but there was something so powerfully pushing away from this woman that I could not bring myself to ask even that simple question.

"And I know what you are going to do with this," she said to me. "You are going to use editing trickery to make it look like we walk together even though we disagree on everything."

"Not me," I said, but by then she was pulling Dora away to continue their walk. "Not me," I added as they left, walking along the river, side by side in the misty rain.

At night we ran the footage of them, talking in different ways but walking together, "every day for years." I said over the picture of them walking away, so close that their elbows touched on every other step, that one of these fine ladies said we would twist everything around so that it looked like they were walking together, even though they lived in opposite worlds. You can see how we twisted the image. Or you can see how there are no edits or trickery, just one steady shot of two women walking together. You can see things any way you want.

There are so many things I don't understand. I think if I met someone who did not like anything I said I would not spend an hour walking with that person every day. And I can't imagine anyone walking with me if they did not like what I said or thought.

And yet Dora and her friend did it, for years. Sorry friend whose name I never got, I don't know why, but you two walking together made me feel good. You must have played some mental trickery on me. That was not fair.

22

A Child's Made Up Story: Mr. Grouchy

This morning Mr. Grouchy got up on the wrong side of the bed. Picture of Mr. Grouchy getting up with a frown.

Yesterday Mr. Grouchy also got up on the wrong side of the bed, but it was the other side. Picture of Mr. Grouchy getting up on that side.

Mr. Grouchy never said "Hello" to anyone. He just mumbled, "I'm having a bad day." Picture: Mr. Grouchy passing smiling people mumbling.

Mr. Grouchy did not believe anything was happy. Pictures of Mr. Grouchy thinking of rain and car crashes, and hitting himself on the finger with a hammer.

Then one day Mr. Grouchy saw a little girl watering a flower growing out of a crack in the sidewalk. Picture of Mr. Grouchy asking the little girl, "Why are you doing that? It will just get stepped on."

The little girl looked up at the frowning Mr. Grouchy while

still watering with her watering can. Picture of little girl saying to Mr. Grouchy, "But until then it will make the sidewalk a happy place."

Mr. Grouchy laughed at her and walked away. Picture of Mr. Grouchy leaving her, shaking his head with little girl watering behind him.

Mr. Grouchy told the story to his secretary. Picture of Mr. Grouchy saying, "Can you believe anything so silly? The little girl thinks a flower makes the sidewalk a happy place."

Secretary smiles. Picture of secretary saying, "Mr. Grouchy, thank you. That is the nicest story. I will tell it to my friends."

Mr. Grouchy sits alone in his office. "Humph," he thinks. "I made my secretary happy. I think that makes me feel happy."

Mr. Grouchy goes back to little girl. "I never felt happy before. Can I help you water the flower?" Picture, the last picture, of Mr. Grouchy watering the flower and smiling.

The End, or as they often say in children's books, The Beginning.

One day, one story. No overdue fines at the library. You can make up the stories if you just see a man and a little girl looking at a tiny flower growing in the sidewalk.

23

The PNE is A Hundred

Ten years ago I did a story about the last prize home being built at the Pacific National Exhibition. This would be the last year for the fair—the city wanted to get rid of the decaying, boring amusement park.

Nine years ago I did a story about the last prize home. The fair did not vanish as was predicted the year before, but this year it would.

Eight years ago I refused to call it the last prize home. The fair was coming back. From looking like a threadbare old-timer with nothing new to entertain the folks, the fair was changing. I was appalled when they knocked down a row of buildings along East Hastings on the south of the fair and put up a park with a pond and a little bridge. I like ponds and bridges, but I like the PNE more. And I was even more upset when they knocked down more buildings on Renfrew Street to put up another park, this one with fountains and statues.

The fair was now a vest-pocket of what it had been, but on the other hand, it was looking good, and rejuvenated and fun. It took on a Disneyland atmosphere, with a parade a couple of times a day and litter picker-uppers working all day, every day. Clean, wholesome and, again, fun.

More people came. Those who had not been to the fair for years were coming back, mainly because their neighbours said it was getting so good. It was crowded—of course there was less area to walk on so the crowd was more condensed—but crowds at a fair make it fun.

I gave credit to the management and directors and everyone who was working to make it better. But then a couple of cameramen at different times said the same thing.

"You know, it's Laura Ballance who made this happen."

Laura Ballance, the sexy-looking, hard-working public relations director of the fair. She was the one who promoted the new rides, who defended the need for the fair and promoted the history, and who is the spokeswoman whenever something goes wrong—because no matter where you are, something always goes wrong. But Laura can change a disaster into a triumph and make you want to come back for more.

Laura Ballance, whom I knew as a despondent, grossly overweight, single mother who had been fired from her job fifteen years earlier and thought she would have to go back to being a waitress at night or maybe ask for government help because you can't be a waitress when you have two small girls at home.

When I saw her walking to work now she was coming from the far side of the parking lot. She was slim.

"How did you do that?" I asked.

"Do what?"

"You know, that," I said, looking at that.

"Eat less."

There you go, every diet book in the world in two words.

"How do you keep it off?"

"Eat less."

I followed her to her office just outside the gate of Playland, next to the roller coaster. The door had a sign: LB Media Group.

Inside was her staff of ten, all busy, all saying good morning to their employer, all more than happy to be working for her. She started her company with just herself.

"She's amazing." "She never quits." "Of all the public relations people I have ever worked for she is the best, by far."

I followed her into her office and she already had two phones going. I learned then that she has been working since six a.m., four hours before she got to work. She would put in another ten hours.

"This is a busy time of the year," she said.

It is also busy during the Boat Show, for which she handles the public and media relations, and the Car Show and the Cloverdale Rodeo and the Woman's Show and, recently, she was in charge of half the media who showed up for the Olympics, the ones who did not have accreditation.

That was probably the hardest job since the non-accredited reporters who land at the airport and take a cab to town expecting everything to be available to them are the worst to deal with. After all, "I am from blah, blah, the leading blah, blah, magazine, newspaper, on-line purveyor of blah, blah. Don't you know how important I think I am?

"I did not have time to get any accreditations. So I need lots of help."

They are not easy folks to satisfy. The fact that they did not bother to get accredited has nothing to do with the level of their own self-importance. "But you still have to treat them like royalty," said Laura. "They will be writing stories and shaping opinions."

We walked across the grounds of the PNE and she said she had met a man whom she thought I could do a story about.

He was Japanese and she saw him one morning standing outside the horse barn. She stopped to talk. That is a sign of a brilliant woman, just stopping to say hello.

He told her that as a boy he had been held as a prisoner in that barn when the police came and took away his family's home and fishing boat and told them to pack a suitcase and come with them. He was born in Canada but he was under arrest because his name and his face were Japanese and Canada was now at war with Japan.

He did not say, but I have often wondered why the Germans in Canada and America were not put into prison camps during the war. The answer of course was as clear then as now, although no one said it. The Germans were the same race as most Canadians and Americans.

We have come a long way. Thankfully, Afghani-Canadians are allowed to be free.

But during World War II the PNE was closed while it was turned into a prison camp. And it was also closed during World War I when it was a staging ground and marching field for soldiers going off to Europe.

Except for that, it has never missed a year. In 1910 it was a brave new idea to have a country fair, which those in charge said would be an Industrial Exhibition, because who really would go to see homemade jams and pies when everyone made jams and pies at home.

So they came to marvel at the telephone and the cars, but mostly it was the rides and the ice cream that got them to stay. The problem was, "You want to go all that way just for some ice cream and to look at a telephone, which we don't need and will never need?"

That is because the fair was opened in a place so far from the city that it would take a couple of hours to get there by car, and half a day by horse. There was no other way. It was in the sticks and getting there was more of an adventure than being there.

So to help people travel, the city put in a streetcar line that ran along East Hastings and ended at the fair. With the streetcars came people, who were daring enough to live that far from downtown Vancouver. Up went the large, pointy-roofed houses on Victoria Drive, which folks could now get to on the tram. And up sprang Commercial Drive with its butcher shops and dress stores. It became so popular that it got its own streetcar line branching off from East Hastings.

The same thing happened when the Sky Train went to Metro Town and another line went along Lougheed Highway to North Road. Everywhere a station was built high-rise condos followed.

Across the street from the fair on Renfrew Street adventurous people built houses. "Look, dear, we can live in the country and I can get to work on the streetcar."

All of the original PNE prize homes were moved into that neighbourhood. They look like most of the other houses around there, small bungalows, very well made, no leaks, and they are still lived in.

In the 1920s and '30s the fair looked like a travelling gospel show. My favourite picture from that era is the Church Of England Tea Tent, with about twenty women with long, starched white dresses standing outside the tent inviting sinners or anyone else inside. Life was pure, and from the faces of some of the women you had better be pure, or else.

By the 1950s the fair was a rough, seedy home for travelling carnies. In the old pictures most of the men working there looked like they were out of jail on day passes. Of course most of them weren't, but I wouldn't trust them with my kids.

There is a picture from then of three small boys in the cockpit of an airplane. They do not look like this is going to be a good experience. The plane is held up by large hooks attached to U-shaped brackets, one at the front and one at the back. The boy in front has his hand on the bracket. If the hook were to slide that way instead of the other he would not have landed with all his fingers.

But most worrisome to me are the two men in charge of the ride. Both have fedoras, both have old ties, threadbare sweaters and wrinkled jackets. Every man dressed the same then, except those who worked in the bank and wore pressed suits. Those who went to rob the bank looked like the carnies behind the airplane. One has a cigarette behind his ear. The other looks like he is glancing around for the police. Bon voyage, kids.

But that has all changed. The ride operators now are mostly working their way through university and their training manuals say SMILE, no matter what. The spirit is up, the mood is friendly, the cotton candy melts on the tongue or in the rain and Laura Ballance makes sure that every positive story gets told.

She is a genius at promotion, a natural, a magician at sending out the good stories, and what the PNE needed was promotion. Those are the stories that bring more visitors.

"How did you do all this?" I asked. "I mean the weight, the job, the success stories with your clients, how?" Just as an added bit of info, she lost more than ninety pounds.

"I wanted to, so I did it. That's all."

You can't beat that.

Then she met her two daughters for a walk around the grounds and some lemonade, something else you can't beat.

"When they were younger they thought I owned all the rides," she said. "They used to go to school and say they had the best mommy in the world."

You definitely can't do better than that.

24

The King of Cassiar

Aman many thought was homeless had more than a hundred people at his funeral. How did that happen?

If you crossed the Ironworkers Memorial Bridge anytime during much of the last decade you saw Gerry. He was waving, and if you slowed down and your window was open he'd say, "Hiya, how you doing, good looking?" And then he'd wave you on your way.

He never asked for money. He never held up a sign that said, Hungry, Homeless, Need Money For Food.

He just smiled and joked and waved and held up his fingers in the peace sign and cleaned the street. He was there in the rain, with a yellow slicker, in summer with a baseball cap and high-vis vest (he followed all the WorkSafe rules) and in winter, walking in the snow on his concrete island between the rivers of traffic.

And then one day in early 2010 he was gone. People looked, but you don't know. What happened to him? He's always there. What do you imagine happened? Don't know. Is there anyone we can call? Who would know? Don't know. And you and I drove on past the island that was empty.

Someone else showed up, holding a sign saying, Homeless, Hungry. He waved in a weak imitation of Gerry. No one gave him money. He was not Gerry. He was on Gerry's corner and he was not Gerry.

Then I got a phone call from a friend of Gerry's. "He's dead," he said.

"Tell me more," I said.

"Don't know nothing, but he had a girlfriend."

"Who?" I did not know this.

He told me. Michelle Stitchman. She lived across the street from Oppenheimer Park where drug deals outnumber the blades of grass.

I had done four stories on Gerry for the television news. He was wonderful. He was so cheerful and friendly and happy. But I knew nothing of his personal life and he told me nothing. When I asked he would turn and start waving to drivers.

Michelle was in her apartment crying. She had cried for four days since Gerry died. They had met by accident and were friends for a few years before he moved in. Before that he lived in the Catholic Charities hostel. Michelle and Gerry became lovers. Yes, people on skid row can be lovers. People with more than twenty-five years separating them can become lovers. People with no money and no jobs and no prospects for the future can become lovers.

I only knew that in the last few years of talking to Gerry he had been very happy.

I did one more story for the news about Gerry. His obituary. Michelle said she loved him and we used old pictures of him waving and picking up cigarette butts and saying, "Sometimes when it hurts inside you have to smile to cover it up."

I didn't know why he said that, at least not at the time he said it. I learned from Michelle that he had liver cancer, which spread to his stomach and lungs. That hurts. But he never told me about the cancer, only about covering up something with a smile.

Michelle knew little of his past, except that he came from Winnipeg and he liked horses and the racetrack. I knew that because I like horses and the racetrack and every time I was there I saw Gerry. I also knew he was no better at picking winners than me, which made me like him better. I don't like people who win at the track. There is something inhuman about them.

The obituary went on the air. If not for that phone call to me his death might have gone unnoticed, because who do you call to find out what happened to a man who many, or most, thought was homeless?

The next day Pete McMartin of the *Vancouver Sun* called me. He is a good guy and a good reporter.

Most reporters would ignore a good story rather than admit he or she had gotten it from another reporter.

Pete did not know about Gerry. He lives to the south of Vancouver. Gerry was a fixture for those who drove north. He was part of the lives of those who use the bridge dedicated to the ironworkers who died building it.

Pete went through the Winnipeg phone book and came up with one of Gerry's sons.

What he learned was more than I knew after a dozen talks with Gerry.

Gerry's son told Pete his father was a neat guy, a wonderful father, the life of the party, and then he had a bad car accident. His head went through the windshield. They put a metal plate in where part of his skull should be.

And then everything changed.

Gerry became forgetful. He was no longer attentive. He stopped being a good father. He left home, left his children and wife. That happens. Life is not fair. Half of you reading this grew up without either fathers or mothers. I did. You did. It happens.

Gerry turned up at Cassiar and Hastings.

He had two sons, Jayson and Jeffrey, and through the grape-vine of hearsay and rumour and gossip they heard he was living on skid row in Vancouver. They heard he was homeless and was a heroin addict and had AIDS.

Both sons have done well. Both showed up at the funeral in suits, both well groomed. Jayson, the older, was vice-president of a company that sells food-processing equipment.

"I came to Vancouver two or three times a year," he said. And when he was here he hunted for his father. He rented a car and drove up and down East Hastings, after he asked where the drug addicts are. He drove and looked and searched and did not see his father.

He did not know that thirty blocks away his father was making thousands of people happy. Jayson had no idea that East Hastings continues out of skid row and goes to the PNE and the racetrack and a world far from the social devastation he was looking at.

While he was searching his father was waving. They never met.

I gave the eulogy at the funeral. I was supposed to be the only speaker because in sad truth, outside of Michelle, as far as anyone knew, I knew him better than anyone else. I had spent much time with Gerry.

I looked out at the audience in the funeral home of glum, sad, tearful faces. What else would you expect to see?

This was the time to invoke the spirit of Gerry:

"You know what Gerry would say, right now, to all of you? All of you with the sad faces and frowns?

"Hiya. How you doing? Have a good day. Hey, handsome. Hello, pretty lady. Drive safe.' That's what Gerry would say."

When the words came out, the image was in my head of a waving man. "Thousands of people, no, tens of thousands, were made happy by him. Gerry had better ratings than CBC.

Basically all of North Vancouver as well as everyone going to the PNE and the racetrack would get a daily dose of feel good from him.

"How you doing? Take care of the children."

You started out sad. Something bad had happened to you. The cure? Take a drink or drive by Hastings and Cassiar. "Hey, big guy. Let's have a smile. Try it. Looks good on you."

Of course some would pass by and say, "I'm not playing this guy's game. That old crazy fool. I'm not going to wave to him. I'm not."

And then the poor sourpuss got stopped by the light. "Damn. He's right out there. But I won't look." Sourpuss looked down at his speedometer saying to himself, "I am not going to talk to that nut case."

Sourpuss looked down at the number zero.

Tap, tap. On his window. He looks up. Gerry is smiling. It was not an academy award-type winning smile. It was a real, honest smile. Gerry's grin could melt a frozen sourpusses.

Through the closed window: "How you doing, young fellow. You have a good day."

Young Sourpuss was killing himself trying not to smile, but he lost. I saw him. I was standing on the corner watching and I saw Sourpuss smile. Gerry was magic.

In winter he built his snowmen on the island and decorated the metal pole at the end of it to look like a Christmas tree. On Valentine's Day he put up paper hearts.

He was not just an institution. He was a soul, a spirit, waving and making you feel good. He never asked for anything.

And that traffic island, my god, it was almost impossible to walk on. It was so steeply sloped that my ankles were killing me after ten steps. Gerry spent ten years walking back and forth a hundred times a day.

It was his world. He kept it clean and safe and joyful.

One of the neatest things he did was save a lot of drivers a pile of money, maybe even their lives. The sign that warned the island was ahead was knocked down one night in an accident. That meant there was no warning for drivers coming up to a hunk of concrete nine inches high. In metric that's about from your wrist to your elbow. Those who hit it at night had their steering wheels ripped out of their hands and one of their front wheels slammed up into the fender.

One morning Gerry showed me ten hubcaps that he had collected from around the island from the night before. When you drive into something that hard it will wreck your car and may overturn you.

Gerry called city hall. He used a quarter that someone had given him and called from a phone across the street near McDonald's where he got his coffee.

No one did anything. He called again. And again. And the next day with a dozen more hubcaps in his collected pile he called again. He showed me the hubcaps and said something had to be done. I agreed. But city hall was doing nothing.

The next day Gerry did something. He got some lumber and reflective tape from somewhere in Vancouver. I suspect from a construction site. And he got on a bus with his boards and tape and rode across town and built his own warning sign. No more crashes.

A day later the city put up a sign.

"Now he's gone," everyone said.

Except he's not. Because I know, and you know, there are thousands of folks who pass that spot every day and say, "Hiya, Gerry. How you doing? You have a good day now, you hear." Gerry is still standing there. Just drive by and look.

Then Jayson spoke to those at the funeral. He was not expected to speak. He was eloquent. He had been ashamed of his father.

He had avoided telling his children about their grandfather. But now he was at a gathering of people who had come to celebrate his father's life.

He did not know that his father had brought joy to so many. He did not know his father was a legend in Vancouver.

He did not know that his father had said, "How you doing, young lady," to Reverend Donna Millar. He did not know the minister had volunteered to do the service at his memorial because she liked him.

"He called me a young lady," she said. "I have grandchildren. Do you know how good he made me feel?"

He did not know that the funeral home had given him the space and time with no charge. The director liked Gerry.

Jayson knew nothing of this. He learned it all at his father's funeral.

The last words I said were, "You can tell your children they had a cool grandfather."

Jayson held up his fingers in the peace sign for me.

At the end of the funeral Rev. Millar played Louis Armstrong's famous song, "What a Wonderful World."

Everyone cried as they always do at a funeral when that is played. "What a Wonderful World" played for someone who is no longer in this world is a heartbreaker.

Six hours later my wife and I were babysitting at our house for our granddaughters. I always listen to 650 CISL because I like the old music.

"What a Wonderful World" came on. Ruby, who was almost six, got up and started dancing.

"That's my favourite song," she said. "The teacher plays it in my ballet class."

She did a twirl.

"That song makes everyone happy," she said.

That is the way life works. If you can't find the answer, wait.

25

Funny Faces

We are now entering deep into the publishing world of children's books.

The publisher says, "We need something that will make them laugh, even if they can't read."

The writer says, "I can try to write something funny but it will have twists and turns and if they can't read it will not be funny."

The meeting goes on for hours with old heads trying to think of young ideas. Something basic, simple and funny.

"Horse meets a goat?"

"So what?"

"Little old lady swallows a fly?"

"Been done."

"Blaaaaaaa," says little boy who is sitting in a chair at the back of the publisher's meeting. He is accompanying his father because it is Bring Your Child To Work Day, even if you know your child will be bored.

"Don't do that," said the father.

"Uggggggghhhh."

The boy has his fingers up his nose and with the other hand is pulling up his eyebrows.

"Aaaaaahhhhhgggh."

"Kennedy, I said don't do that, there are people here, and my boss. They'll see you."

"Flubbbbbbba."

Kennedy has now sucked in his cheeks and crossed his eyes.

"Did you see that, chief? That is funny," said the writer.

"Oooooogggghha."

Kennedy has twisted his ears back and sucked in his lips.

"Come here," said Kennedy's father. "You are going to get a spanking."

"Nooooo," said the publisher, or the writer. If you are a writer, always give credit to the publisher.

"He has saved us."

Out comes the book: Kennedy's Funny Face. The plot is simple. Kennedy was having a boring day and then decided to do something harmless and funny and infectious and just plain neat, and it worked. By the end of the book everyone is laughing and the boring day is gone.

One last word from Kennedy: "Waaaaaahhhhhga," he said with his middle fingers inside his mouth stretching his cheeks apart and his index fingers stretching his eyes. That is not easy to do without practice.

Okay, none of the above happened. But I was with a cameraman one day when we could find nothing. We looked behind things and over other things and…you know the drill. We looked everywhere and then we saw a little boy making faces at a little girl.

"Oh my story god in notebook heaven. Look!" said the cameraman. If you are a reporter always give credit to the photographer, and the editor. They probably deserve it anyway so don't hesitate. In fact, as a general rule, always give credit to others if they do anything. It will help get everything done.

We interrupted. "Can we talk to your son, and would you make that funny face for us again?"

From there we hit gold in face after face. Everyone except one made a face that made us and them and others passing by laugh. It was magic. Stretch a cheek, pull an ear, cross an eye, and some that made gross descriptive sounds that made others laugh. That was all there was to it. The day had a memory and was saved by a little boy who made a funny face.

But it almost did not happen for us.

"Would you do that again for us?" we asked after we first saw him and after we had asked his mother, "May we ask him?"

"Yes," she said.

"No," he said.

"Why?" we asked.

"It's embarrassing. I don't want to do it," he said.

"Please." We thought, while our only hope was shutting the door and leaving us out.

"No," he said and he left. At that moment I thought the story god had been toying with me, just building me up to drop me. But check out Rule Number One.

"Well, let's try someone else," said the cameraman.

We did and everything was perfect.

On the last page of the real life children's book: Little boy saying "NO" is just a starting point. Also, what do kids really know about the value of funny faces? They just make them, but adults are smart enough to capitalize on them.

P.S. Thanks, little boy. It would have never happened if you hadn't done what you did not want us to see you doing.

26

Kids on First Avenue

Before the Olympics, First Avenue at the corner of Quebec Street was dull. Along where the Olympic Village now stands the street was boring, dusty and dull. There was a lot of traffic, but it was just going by, getting from somewhere to somewhere else. It was very dull.

On one side of the street were abandoned warehouses with an abandoned streetcar track running in front of them. On the other side were more abandoned warehouses and a couple of car fix-it places. You could hunt for many words to describe it, but dull would do fine.

Until...look at that group of kids coming this way, now stopping: "Honk! Honk! Come on. Honk!"

And then a driver honked back.

Cheers. As much as the first breath of a baby is followed by cries, a class of grade seven kids had created life above the concrete.

"Honnnnk."

More cheers. They pumped their arms like they were pulling an air horn on a truck and "Honnnnk!" the trucker pulled his air horn.

Applause.

The kids were so polite. They stood with their toes up to the steel tracks, but not one step beyond. There were thirty or more of them, waving and honking and cheering.

"We were tired," said one of the adults. They had been on a field trip to Science World and had come down here to stretch their legs. But the legs, at least of the adults, got worn out, "so we stopped to rest, and now we can't get them to leave."

Tired? Kids? No. The miracle of childhood happened when they stopped because that's when play began.

"What do you do for joggers?"

"Clop, clop."

"And bikes?"

"Ring, ring."

Imagine if the education system could keep up with kids.

"Okay, one more," said the teacher, "and then we leave."

"Honk, ring."

"How do you feel when they honk back?"

"Good. We like them."

"And if they don't?"

"Boo, no fun."

"One more, then we really have to go," said the teacher.

"Honnnnk, clop, clop, ringggggg." And right on cue, they got a honk and a ring and a thumbs-up over the clopping. Cheers.

They got in three or four more despite the teacher's orders. They are not perfect children. And then they left and the street went back to boring and dull and dusty with traffic going from somewhere to somewhere else, without horns, without thumbs, without little bells on handle bars. It was just a street. The miracle was gone. But for the time they were there, the kids were magicians. They were given a dull street and turned it into a game. It was a shame they had to go back to school. They had so much to teach before they got there.

The Ten Gallon Hat

27

I t isn't the same, I said to myself. It is all plastic in a plastic
world. Of course I don't believe that. There is just more
plastic in the world than I like.

I was at the Cloverdale Rodeo and looking at hats, cowboy
hats, and so many of them were plastic. They were mostly white,
cloth, preformed with curled up sides and then sprayed with
plastic. They would not flop even in the rain, which they would
never see because those who wear those hats would not go out in
the rain. But probably the most appealing thing about them was
they were selling for $20.

I saw a real cowboy sitting on a horse. On the cowboy was a
beautiful, black Stetson as large as...I was going to say Texas but
BC is much bigger. It was a hat as big as the most beautiful province. It was his parade riding hat, he said.

"How much, may I ask?"

He pushed up the front brim with a massive finger.

"Five hundred dollars," he drawled.

I gulped. For a hat? One hat?

"What do you get for $500?" I asked.

"A hat that you're not going to let fall off your head." He laughed, then rode away.

That was a cowboy answer.

Then I saw another cowboy, standing near the pens where they mount the broncos and then try to hold on for half a minute. He had the most beaten-up, misshapen, torn and ragged hat I had seen all day. That was a real cowboy hat.

"Hi, pretty nice hat."

Suddenly I realized I was walking up to a cowboy who had a body that looked like it was made of steel, which had been broken in numerous places, and had no fat or softness about him and he had knuckles on his hands that were larger than some people's hands and I was saying, "Nice hat."

I hoped he did not take it wrong.

"Yup," he said.

He looked me up and down. I had no hat, even though the sun was hot. I had no boots. I had no jeans and no stitching on my shirt. I was a city boy in cowboy country.

"Do you mind if we take a picture of your hat?"

"It's nothing fancy," he said, "but sure. But I only have a couple of minutes before I ride."

A couple of minutes is eternity if you find the right hat and his was the gateway to all the time in the world.

We took pictures. He took it off. "It's been stomped on more times than I can count," he said while rolling it around in his hands. "It's been used as a pillow. It's been dragged through the mud. It's a pretty good hat."

His name was Waylon Wasylciw, from Montana. He was 26 years old and he was a professional cowboy, riding the circuit like professional golfers follow the circuit. The difference is golfers can make a lot of money and the only thing that can get hurt is their pride. They also wear golf caps supplied by golf club companies with the company's logo on the front.

Cowboys get crushed ribs and concussions and broken arms and broken fingers and broken legs. They make very little money, or less. And they supply their own hats.

Waylon started putting on a protective vest that looked like a bullet proof shield that police wear. Cowboys are not getting soft, they just want to last a little longer so they can ride a few more times.

He said he paid $150 for his hat about three years ago. "It looked good then. But you know the best thing about this hat? I won two buckles and two jackets after I got it. It's my good luck hat."

I did not ask how much the buckles and jackets were worth, because the way he said it I knew they were worth more than money. He turned the hat around and showed us the Jack Daniel's patch on the front. We had seen it earlier and taken a picture of it. "That makes it official," he said.

The announcer said bronco riders should get ready.

"How long does a hat last?"

"Well, this one I promised to give to a little kid, so this one's going very soon."

I was shocked. How can you give away a good luck hat?

"There was this little kid I saw last year in a small rodeo in Alberta. He asked me if I would give him my hat. I couldn't say no, but I said next year. That's this year."

The announcer called his number, 4, which was written on a cloth vest that he put over his bullet- and hoof-proof vest.

"Gotta go," he said.

We watched him climb over the boards and settle onto the saddle. Then he wrapped the bridle around the knuckles on his right hand and grabbed the horn of the saddle.

"Ready."

That was his last and only word before they opened the chute and the horse was out with all hoofs off the ground and then it came down with Waylon off the saddle. The horse hit the dirt and Waylon slammed onto the hard leather and then the horse was up again and Waylon's head was back near the tail and his feet were up above the neck of the horse.

The black felt hat was on the ground and the rear left hoof of the horse came down on it and as the hoof came up again the hat went flying into the air and it was still going up when Waylon crashed again into the saddle and fell off. The rear hooves came down a hand width away from his head, which had no protection.

Clowns came running out and another rider raced over to grab the bucking horse and Waylon got up, grabbed his hat, slapped it against his leg and put it on his head while he limped off the range of the rodeo cowboy.

You have the right to think that rodeos are cruel to animals. I am not going to defend them or criticize them. They are a way of life that is harsh and tough, to the cowboys also. I am not going to stand on the sidelines and say to anyone you should not do what you do because some think you should not do it.

Race horses are well fed, well cared for and live short lives. And I love going to the track.

The horses in the RCMP's Musical Ride stand in their stalls between rides not moving, barely blinking. They are trained so tightly there is nothing but obedience left. I love the Musical Ride. So does most of this country. I feel sorry for the horses.

Rodeos are a rugged way to make a living. You have to get your body broken and then listen to the criticism of others who can't do what you do saying you should not do it.

Waylon came back to us. He was like a golfer who had just shot par. His finish depended on how others finished.

"Are you really giving away your hat?"

He took off his heavy vest. He was already over a beating that would have sent most of us to hospital and then a week off work.

"Have to," he said. "I said I would and I will. That's the next stop."

It takes a big man to wear a big hat, but it takes someone even bigger not to wear it.

28

The Hanging Garden and How it Got There

"Y ou've got to see this. It is the most beautiful garden I've ever seen." That was John McCarron, a cameraman I have worked with in many beautiful gardens, so this one must be pretty good.

"And there's almost nothing in the ground," he added.

We drove to 19th Avenue near Victoria Drive. It was just a small city lot, but it looked like Babylon, or at least what I imagine the ancient city looked like when it had enough hanging gardens to make it one of the wonders of the world.

We entered the front gate between rows of pots of blooming geraniums. Many pots, many blooms, and all of them under homemade plastic roofs to protect them from the rain.

A man was sitting on the front steps. He looked content. He had a smile. I would smile, too, if I was looking at this.

"Hello," followed quickly by, "This is amazing."

"Who told you about this?" he asked.

"He," I said, pointing to John who had his camera. "He said it was the most beautiful garden ever."

After you say something like that you usually get invited onto the property.

He told us his name was Joe Zenz. He had a German accent, he introduced us to his wife who was very sweet and then said, "If you like this, come look at the backyard."

Ten, no, thirty, no, fifty hanging baskets, all geraniums. Wait, follow him around the corner of his house. Almost a hundred more hanging baskets, all geraniums. The beauty was instant and overwhelming. Joe was humble and thankful for the compliments.

He said he paid nothing for them, they were all grown from cuttings and seeds. He just happened to like geraniums and the flowers lasted from spring to fall—not bad for a cost-nothing garden. He did not plant them in the ground because there was not enough room to have this many flowers.

He had been a baker for Safeway, but after he retired, he said, his wife did all the baking and he did all the planting. "It is my life," he said, the same as many gardeners say. And when they say that they make the world a better place.

It never occurred to me how come the garden was here. How come on this street in this city and country such a beautiful thing was created. I just accepted that. I knew he was an immigrant from his German accent. I am an immigrant. So is half of this country.

You don't ask, "How come you are living here?" on the first visit when you are being shown a work of beauty. You admire the beauty. In fact, if you think of anything else you are not admiring as much as enquiring. That may be legitimate, but it is being a bit nosy.

I thanked him and we put the story on television and many

people called asking how they could grow the same kind of garden and asking where he lived, and he had been kind and said tell them all, let them see.

Just another gardening story.

A few weeks later I was out with my German friend, Gunther Blasig. I have written about him many times. He escaped from East Germany when being caught meant you would be shot. He started a landscape company in Maple Ridge with a shovel and a shoebox to hold his bills. It is now one of the largest and most respected companies in the province.

He visits terminally ill patients in hospice care with his dogs, bringing them comfort. He did an experiment once with the help of a nurse. They took the blood pressure of a patient dying of cancer. It was through the ceiling. Then he brought in one of his dogs, a standard poodle, big girl, and she put her head on the bed and the patient began petting her. His blood pressure fell and fell, then fell some more.

"I know it works," said the nurse, or maybe Gunther said it. But they both knew it.

Gunther does this a couple of times a week, and he makes pancakes for the Lion's Club Mother's Day morning and he cares for a few other old people, along with a couple of other good deeds. In short, he is a good guy.

I thought he might like to meet Joe and see his landscaping in the sky.

They spoke in German. They spoke for a while. It was obviously not about the geraniums because they were talking without looking up. After they said goodbye and shook hands Gunther said to me, "You would not believe how come he is here."

Joe was in Erwin Rommel's Panzer Division during World War II. It was one of the most famous fighting forces, ever, led by the most famous German field marshal, ever. The hundreds of tanks that roamed North Africa were invincible.

Rommel was the same. He was the only high-ranking German officer who was not indicted for war crimes after the war. He defied Hitler's orders and did not shoot his prisoners, including the captured Jewish soldiers.

He ordered his own troops to cut their rations of water so that their prisoners could drink.

Later in the war he was part of a plot to kill Hitler, a plot that failed. Rommel, of course, was not really invincible. The plot cost him his own life. He is the only German leader from World War II who is still a hero in Germany. To serve under him was an honour. That was Joe.

But nor was the Panzer Division invincible—nothing is. Joe and his tank, along with many others, were captured by General George S. Patton, one of the most famous American generals. Patton led his troop by standing in front of them, even as a general. He got into serious trouble when he slapped a soldier whom he thought was pretending to be sick to get out of fighting.

If you grew up during the war you know Patton helped win it. If you saw the movie about him you know he was one of the most fearless leaders of all time.

The British defeated most of the Panzer Division, but a small part of it was captured by Patton, including Joe's tank.

If you are going to be captured you might as well get the bragging rights to say you were defeated by the best. Joe was sent to a prisoner of war camp in the middle of America. He told Gunther that he had such a peaceful time there, and that his treatment was so good, that after the war he wanted to stay.

He applied to immigrate to America and Canada. Canada answered first.

That's why there were beautiful geraniums on East 19th. Every story has its roots, sometimes starting far away.

Since then the pots have come down. Joe's wife died. Then Joe. We are not invincible, but we can be unforgettable.

Art of Courage

On this one day Fumiko made a mistake. She did not hide deeply enough in the woods to remain undiscovered. On this one day she was behind the branches of a bush, but near a roadway and we could see something moving.

Slowly, cautiously, because we do not want to upset the way the world is working, we moved closer until we could see it was a woman with a sketch pad.

Quietly, we said hello, and excuse us. She was pleasant, not startled, but not outgoing with a big hello in return.

"Hello," she whispered.

We asked if we could interrupt her and would she let us see her pictures. She looked at me and the cameraman and for a moment I thought she would say no, which is her right, and we would respect her privacy and apologize and back off.

She said, "Yes, if you would like to."

Her sketches, in colour, were beyond real. The great artists of our time who make an animal or a flower seem more vivid and real than a photograph help us see what we miss in the world. Fumiko's sketches were the same. She had almost a full pad of sketches, many drawn on both sides of the paper. They were berries and leaves and flowers and stalks and grass and moss and things I had not noticed before.

128

"How many do you have?" I asked.

"I have stacks of pads at home. Maybe a thousand pictures." Then she looked down.

"May we ask, it is sort of rude I know, but why were you hiding in the bush?"

She said she was shy. She suffered from terrible shyness. She usually went deep into bushes to draw where there would never be anyone to look at her work.

"Has anyone seen these before?" I asked.

"No, only my husband, and now you."

"How long have you been doing this?"

"Twenty years."

There are times when you stop because you have no more questions. At that moment I could no longer interfere into a life that wished to be alone. There is no point in me saying, snap out of it girl. Get with the program. Go sell your work and be rich and famous and get your picture on the cover of a magazine.

"There are more people who are shy than you imagine," she said.

"Do you know why you are?" I asked, awkwardly.

"Because it is me, like my face. It is me."

She said there was a conference at UBC on shyness.

"Did you go?"

"No. I was…" and then she said nothing.

"Too shy," I said and she laughed, gently.

She said she did something brave once, and only once. She left Japan, alone, with no relatives or friends in Vancouver and against her parents' wishes.

"That was the only thing I have ever done."

"That was pretty big," I said.

She also married someone here, and now her name was Fumiko Maplethorp. That was something brave. And she showed us her drawings. That was something.

"Will you ever have an art show?"

"Someday, maybe, if they are good enough."

I was looking at art that would sell anywhere.

I never saw Fumiko again, and that was more than ten years ago. But since then many people have said to me, "Do you remember that artist you did a story about who was so shy? I used to be like that. Then one day something happened and everything was good after that."

Someday I will look in an art gallery, or maybe you will, and see pictures of berries and leaves and moss and the name at the bottom will be Fumiko Maplethorp. Buy a picture. You will be holding a work of not just beauty, but courage.

30

So Easy Finding Mr. Wright

W e saw them down on the rocks at low tide behind the Vancouver Aquarium. There was a group of them, which is good enough reason to go and snoop.

They were pleasant, they were from the Aquarium and were releasing salmon fry into Burrard Inlet through a mini stream they had brought back to life. A hundred years ago there were countless streams, hundreds and hundreds, that ran out of Vancouver and Burnaby and North and West Vancouver and all the other towns that touch salt water.

Those were the days when millions of tiny salmon started out life here, and not just schools but mega universities of them returned. Those were the days when farmers would pitchfork returning salmon out of streams and use them for fertilizer. Of course that was not a wise move, but it gives you an idea how plentiful the fish were.

Now there are little more than a dozen active natural streams in the entire lower mainland. There are a growing number of artificial, people-made outlets to the ocean, which is good but some of them are little more than plastic pipes leading to breeding grounds that don't exist. When the fish come back they are scooped out and bred in captivity and then the fry go back into the pipe for their maiden swim.

Can you imagine their conversation on the final run: "Great grandma used to tell the children that it was a wild trip back jumping over rocks and avoiding bears, and it was worth it because at the end we would have terrific sex. But there's not enough room in this pipe to even try to snuggle."

Any attempt to bring back what we threw away is good and we talked for a few minutes to the Aquarium people and watched the fish getting released. But this we have seen before. It is a good story, but even with a good story you still get the "So what?" factor. "So what's new about releasing fish?" "Well, nothing actually, but they are doing it and we should always report good news."

"Good news is boring. If you tell me another airplane landed safely I will punch you in the nose. I know we, the public, are complaining that the media only reports bad news, but honestly, if you only report good news without a new angle we will turn you off and read gossip magazines."

So we skipped doing the fish story. And then as we were leaving we saw him, walking over the rocks picking up garbage. This we have seen many times, and yet this never gets old.

We talked. His name was Mr. Wright. When someone says their name is Mr. or Mrs. something, that is their name. He will never be Joe or Nick. He will always be Mr. Wright. We asked him why he was picking up garbage.

"Because it looks bad," he said.

That is the kind of answer you pray for. He was not doing it because it made him feel good, although that would be fine, and he was not doing it as part of a daily exercise of bending over, which also would have been fine. In fact, that would have been wonderful if he had combined bending with cleaning. Others would have said, "See, I can get something out of picking up garbage. I can lose the fat around my tummy. Of course, the garbage is stinky, so maybe I'll just bend over without picking up anything. But then that would be exercising and I hate to exercise so I'll just watch TV."

It amazes me how many ways we can see anything. But Mr. Wright was doing it to fix a wrong, and that was beautiful. That was the fundamental best answer. He was not a scout leader trying to set a good example or part of an organized group trying to clean the earth on Earth Day, or someone trying to be noticed doing a good deed. If we had not been down on the rocks we would not have seen him from the seawall where most people were walking.

"It looked bad so I picked up a few things," he added.

He looked like he was a banker from England. He had neatly combed grey hair and a trimmed grey moustache. He spoke with eloquent perfection. He was a retired bulldozer driver.

He did not at first want to say how often he did this or for how long. His answers to these questions were, "Fairly often," and "not too long." Eventually he said he started one day when he was seventy and was taking a walk around the seawall. He was now seventy-four. And how often? "I walk around the park every day and if the tide is out I climb down and pick up bottles and broken glass and more junk than you can imagine."

He said he carried a few plastic grocery bags with him and when they were full he climbed back up the stone steps that go down off the wall about every 200 metres and put the bags in a garbage can.

Yes, he did get exercise. Yes, at seventy-four he looked like he was hopping up the stairs. And yes, he would now be noticed for doing a good deed. Hopefully he did inspire others to do the same.

And what was the new twist on a guy picking up garbage? We

have seen that many times. The world has many people who do that same thing for no reason other than to do something good. What made Mr. Wright different from the people sending the baby salmon out into the ocean? Why was his story on the air that night?

Why did the Good Samaritan get a story in the Bible? There are many people who would help someone in need, even if others did not.

The answer is, if you are looking for a good story check out Rule Number Three: Good people make good stories. No matter how many times it is told, it is always good to hear.

31

Momma Knows Best

You know that the railroad made Canada— all of Canada, at least west of Quebec and Ontario, which likes to think of itself as Canada but without the west they would just be snooty places with poutine and politicians.

And you know it was the railroad coming across the country that kept the good people of old-time British Columbia from joining the United States. The railroad did come and everyone was happy, except for the people of Seattle who have to have passports now to go to Whistler.

The lesson is railroads were very powerful, at least back then.

You also know that mother ducks are smart and know where water is, even if you can't see it. And from reading this book you have probably figured out that a duck can lead you to a wonderful story.

On the south side of Malkin Avenue across the street from Strathcona park are rows of wholesale produce warehouses. They stretch for five blocks or more. There is nothing around them but concrete loading bays. And that's where we saw momma duck and her seven little ones, wisely, faithfully, obediently following her.

We had never seen a duck there before.

"Have you ever seen a duck here?" I asked a truck driver as the duck and her kiddies went under his truck.

"Never."

"Have you ever seen this?" I asked a fellow loading lettuce boxes off a truck.

He looked with curiosity and said no.

No one had ever seen a duck here. There is no water. It is not a duck-friendly area. A woman who worked inside brought out a bowl of water. Women do things like that.

The momma duck looked at the offering, then kept going as though she had something else in mind.

Should we call the City Pound, which is around the corner? Should we try to catch them and take them somewhere they might find water (even though catching them would be idiotically impossible—but it was a thought).

Momma duck got her feet tangled in some plastic zap straps that were locked together in circles. It is hard to walk with webbed feet that are handcuffed. She struggled for a minute, then freed herself and her babies followed her.

We watched her for a long time and it was hot and dry and we felt bad and we were worried. She went around the corner of the last building and headed toward the security fence. The chain-link barrier was a thousand feet long and topped with barbed wire. The bottom was driven into the ground.

On the other side of the fence is a vast, barren land of weeds and old train tracks. But it was not always so. A long time ago, while the Canadian Pacific Railroad was stretching across the nation they also managed to gobble up all the good land. They made incredible deals to basically own most of what became Vancouver. Their tracks went along Burrard Inlet and ended at the foot of Granville Street, where they built a magnificent station. They also got much of the nearby forest, which they sold to those who wanted to live here, and the owners of the railroad became very rich, which made them happy.

Later other railroad barons wanted to do the same, but sadly, they were a bit late.

The only route into the new city of Vancouver was along what is now Grandview Highway. The problem was, starting shortly after Boundary Road, the land went uphill. That is not good for trains, which treat hills like sinful places to be avoided.

And there was another problem. Once they got into Vancouver the only land left for them to park their trains on was under water. They looked at a map and there was False Creek, which then was huge.

If you stand now at Science World and look east everything you see was once under water. False Creek continued on from Main Street, where you are standing, all the way to Clark Drive, which is the hill you see at the end of your field of vision almost two kilometres away. That is a lot of water.

All of that land you are looking at, where Sky Train now runs, where the old CN station still stands, where the rail yards are and where the warehouses are, way up to the far end of Terminal Avenue where Home Depot is, was under water. False Creek was massive.

If you drive along Great Northern Way on the southern edge of this area you pass a grassy field named China Creek Park. Back in the days we are talking about China Creek was big enough for a steam-powered tugboat to go from False Creek to Burrard Inlet. Even if you can't picture it, that was a lot of water the Great Northern Railroad was looking at.

So they had two problems: getting their trains to the edge of the water, and filling in the water.

Solution: hire some folks, mostly those lucky Chinese labourers who happened to be in abundance before the country stopped allowing them to come in and then watched while some of its white citizens smashed up their stores. Hire them to do a little digging.

They dug a trench, now called the Grandview Cut. The floor of the trench was level, just made for trains, with very high walls where the hill was still far above them. Now, what to do with the dirt that came out of this excavation?

That was the solution to the second problem. Simply dump the dirt into the water at the end of the trench. Brilliant. Two problems solved with one dump: get rid of the dirt and get rid of the water. As the trench grew, False Creek shrank.

Great Northern began the digging in 1913. But then they had another problem, and this one they could not solve. In 1918 the company went bankrupt and was taken over by the Canadian government, which renamed the line the Canadian National Railroad.

The new owners, financed by taxpayers, finished the work. The new railroad built a magnificent train station with CANA- DIAN NATIONAL engraved across the giant front doors. Trains stopped where there was once water. False Creek ended at Main Street. Warehouses grew up on the sides of the rail yards and now momma duck was leading her children somewhere. She rounded the last warehouse and faced hundreds of feet of fence topped with barbed wire.

Momma headed for one corner where a tiny bit of the fence was pulled up from the ground. She had to flatten herself down to get through it. She did not waddle—it was more like she forced her way between the sharp edges of the steel and the sharp edges of the railroad stones.

Her babies followed. We watched as she walked further and further through the weeds and over the stones and then we could see she was heading toward a large puddle between two rows of tracks. Could she smell it? Could she sense that once there was a great body of water here? It was water where there had once been water. It was a drop where there had been an ocean, but it was enough. It was all momma needed.

What does the duck have to do with the history of the railroad and False Creek?

Nothing, but without the duck the rest of the story is just a history lesson, plopped down in the middle of a school day. "Today, students, we will learn about the formation of Canada. Tomorrow we will forget that and learn about the Industrial Revolution."

To tell the story of False Creek without the duck is interesting, but it has no feeling. To watch a mother duck and her children wandering onto a wilderness of weeds and tracks that once was a mini-ocean of life puts something that comes from the heart into the history. Without the duck all we would have seen is a sad, barren, dry creek that I had passed many times before and I would not have told the cameraman about why it is there.

One other thing. The big CANADIAN NATIONAL words are now covered with VIA. Nothing lasts forever.

32

Polka Dot House

his I don't understand. Of all the things I don't understand—and that includes almost everything outside of
children's books—this I don't understand most of all.

Why don't we ask?

What I mean is I get lots of e-mails and phone calls and in
the old days letters saying, "Right down at the end of my street is
the most wonderful garden in the world in the corner of a con-
demned house with a little old man who is always working on it
and he is always smiling. I wonder why he is smiling? Would you
find out?"

Or.

"I pass this crazy house every day and it has polka dots on it.
Big polka dots. Who lives there? Why would he do that? Would
you do a story on it and put it on television and tell me when you
do so I will know? Thanking you in advance."

Why don't you ask, and then tell me?

If you were to stop and ask they would be happy. And so would
you, and you would have a story to tell and make others happy.

And just to give you a little helping hand and show how
easy it is, we stopped at the polka dot house on Lakewood, in

Vancouver. This is a famous house. If you look up Polka Dot House on the internet you will see several postings saying "This is the coolest house in the city." And, "This house makes Vancouver awesome. I wonder who lives there?"

None of the people writing about it stopped and asked.

It is not hard to find out. The house is painted all white, with large red polka dots of various sizes covering the walls. Some dots are as wide as an arm's length, some two arms.

Knock, knock. Step number one. Next the door opens and a smiling man is standing there. In my case I say, "Hi, I'm from Global television and was wondering…" and before I finish he nods and laughs and says he knows.

Knows what, I want to know? Knows I am from Global or knows what I am wondering? But if I was not from Global television I would still knock on the door and say, "Hi, excuse me, and I know it is none of my business, but you have the coolest house in the city and I was wondering why."

Sincere compliments usually work. And eventually, when I actually do retire, I will continue doing that because when you see a polka dot house you just have to know.

"You're from where?" he asks.

"Global television, thirty years at the end of the news trying to show something nice." Then I add in with my incredulous voice sort of inferring without saying it that you are kidding. "And you don't watch?"

He laughs. "I was just kidding. I've seen you when I've been out at friends' houses. You have to excuse me, but I don't have a TV."

Now I like him even more. He is big and friendly and has a smile that is almost laughter, and no TV. Some people manage without them.

"But I just want to know about…"

"Yes, the house. It is amazing how few people ask," he said.

And then he added, "And you know me."

I looked at him. I stared at him. Please god of memory tell me who he is so I will not embarrass myself. I was still looking when he said, "I'm on your station."

Oh, no, this is worse. He is a new anchor and I have not seen him. He is a fellow reporter, but I don't get into the office much. He is someone I must know, and don't.

"You're Chuck Currie," said Tony Clark, the cameraman who had come up the stairs wondering why I did not act surprised when the door opened.

"Hello," I say, not having a clue who Chuck Currie is.

"White Spot," said Tony, hitting me in the ribs to wake up my brain. "The great commercials. You know, right?"

Uh oh. Fear grips my mind, like when I have to remember someone's name and can't. Because if they were on television I probably did not see it. I watch the news because that is my life. My wife loves the Weather Channel, and the home decorating channels, and if I forget to record *Survivor* for her she would kill me, literally.

But I would rather be on Commercial Drive having coffee and surrounded by a living reality show where I once met someone wearing their pants for a shirt with the seat doubling as a hoodie and I asked, "Excuse me, it is none of my business, but why do you have your arms in your legs?"

And then she said, "I am starting a new trend. I am the first. In a week or two I will be rich. And then I will give away the money because money causes problems."

You cannot make up people like that. And I went home and told my wife that I met someone wearing her pants over her head. And she said, "Rupert got voted off tonight on *Survivor*. I am so sad." And she told me about Rupert and I was sad because Rupert is a nice guy and has come into the lives of millions.

142

During breakfast I told her again about the pants over the head woman and she said that was a dumb thing to do. But she went to work and told someone else about the pants over the head woman because everyone already knows about Rupert and at the pre-school where she works my wife had the best story.

So I stay away from television. But Chuck was gracious and I suddenly remembered those commercials for White Spot, which they run during the news, and I put one and one together and said with gushing admiration: "Those are great. And you ride a bike all over France or the Okanagan."

And then Chuck said he loves polka dots and hence the house is covered with polka dots. And then I know that the happy character in the commercials is real because you cannot be anything except a neat happy guy if you have red spots on your white house.

And then the story keeps growing. He says he loves music. He is in and has organized several bands and other musical groups. Would we like to hear him play the sax?

Yes!

So outside the polka dot house Chuck Currie, who is renowned as a chef and comic performer, played the horn and played it so well I thought what need is there to go on about the polka dot house and the commercials, which would take away time from our television story about his playing.

"Are you crazy?" said Ron Tupper, the editor. "You want to do a story about a guy who lives in a polka dot house and makes funny commercials and leave out the house and the commercials? And they pay you?"

"Well, not leave them out, just minimize them."

"Minimize your head, which God has already done," said Ron.

I like Ron. He wears shorts in the winter and has his wife's picture on his cellphone so when it rings he looks and says, "Isn't she pretty?" You can't beat a guy who defies the cold and warms to his lover. He also sees what is obvious more clearly than me.

"Of course," I said, because the editor is always right. "Plenty of commercial, plenty of dots." Later I take credit for that, and that's insane.

If you go into television—or most other fields—keep that in mind. The one who gets the credit is not usually the one who deserves it.

But for the story: Knock, knock. That's all it took. Maybe Chuck would not have played for me had we not had a camera there. But it would still have been an amazing story. Whoever knocked would have met the star of those amazingly funny commercials. And since then I have watched the commercials and said to everyone who is with me, usually my wife, "I know that guy. Well, at least I met that guy. And he lives in this…"

"I know," she says, "he lives in a polka dot house. But I still feel bad that Rupert got voted off."

I wonder if Chuck feels bad about Rupert. I think I'll ask the next time I pass the dots.

And as for the garden in the corner of the house that someone else asked about. Yes. I did find out about that. That was at the project at 33rd and Main. A story earlier in this book takes place there and you will get to know many things about Vancouver's projects for the poor people.

But yes, he was a man who planted the most wonderful garden in the corner of the social housing complex. He had pails and buckets and flowers and plants everywhere.

He brought his wife into the garden every day, when the sun fell on it. He told her about the flowers and the herbs and the new growth and the old leaves that were dying and she would say, "beautiful."

She was totally blind.

144

The Neighbourhood Olympics

33

Y ou have to practise. You can't have a major event like the opening ceremonies without at least one rehearsal.

And even the rehearsal was the best Olympic event I had been to or seen, and it had only an audience of one dog and one man, and they only saw the tail end of it.

When my wife and I got home on a Sunday night after a long day of standing in lines and spending nine dollars for a German sausage, our neighbours were coming out onto the street. I am lucky. My neighbours are neat—they celebrate the birthdays of the garbage men and have parties in their driveways, and when their pets die they have dignified ceremonies. It is like a small town on one block.

Just across a big bridge was a city feeling its oats. The big O games were everywhere. The crowds were everywhere. The VIPs were everywhere. But on our little street something small and amazing was emerging from the doorways.

145

Barb Rennie had spent the day making banners and tying Chinese lanterns to poles because it was also Chinese New Year. There were hearts everywhere, on banners and paper cut-outs on windows because it was Valentine's Day. And there would now be a parade, a practice parade, because the Olympics were still on their way to this street.

Four couples and five kids, including a new foster child who is living with Caroline and Perry, gathered in the darkness. A parade needs music so Barb played her violin. "O Canada" was sung and played and thirteen people from grade two to retirement walked for almost one entire block. There is only one old street light on a pole at the end of our block. They headed for it. My wife and I joined in. You don't get a parade every day and you should never pass up an opportunity. Beth and Bruce carried a banner that said Fun For All And All For Fun, which *should* be the motto of the Olympics. Alice and Kate, who were both seven, carried the poles with the banners of hearts on them. Jimmy, who is sixteen, gave up a night with his friends to march and sing. And Jimmy's father, Jim, tried to keep everyone going in a straight line. "No, kids, the parade is this way."

Every parade needs the media so Isobel borrowed her mother's camera and flashed away and tried to both be in the parade and take pictures of it.

And every parade needs someone to watch it. Caroline knocked on the door of another neighbour but no one was home. Then she saw a fellow walking down the street with his dog.

"Stop a minute. You can watch," she said.

But he was already slowing because this was more than just a walk with his dog.

"What's your name?"

"Jeff," he said, but he said nothing else.

What do you say when you see a parade in the dark with a

violin and banners and someone trying to keep everyone together but totally failing on a dark street after seven p.m.?

In fifteen seconds the parade had passed him because basically it was only twenty seconds in length. Jeff and his dog disappeared into the darkness, but he had a good story to bring home.

Besides the participants, he was the only witness to the least expensive opening ceremonies of all. It cost nothing and did not change any traffic flow. It did not increase taxes or have any line-ups. It drizzled a bit but no one said they needed a roof, and the lack of snow just made walking easier. As far as a legacy goes, a couple of grade two girls will still be talking about the Olympics they were in when the 2050 or 2070 winter games are messing up traffic and going over budget and fighting the weather.

But that was just practice, because after that things got really good.

A week later, on a Sunday morning when the rain stopped and the sun came up and everyone could see what they were doing, the parade was held again, but this time they kept going into the main event. This was no warm-up. This was the real thing.

Two teenage boys stopped to watch. The audience was swelling. The parade ended and Bruce Bourdon, a high school counsellor, lit a garden torch and gave it to his neighbour's daughter, Alice. She crossed to the middle of the street, which in grade two is halfway across her world. There she met her closest friend in the entire world, Kate, who lives next door to her. Two seven-year-olds touched the tops of their garden torches together while their parents stayed close to make sure they were safe, and the flame was passed from the south side of the street to the north. It was almost at its destination.

Kate carried the torch five steps to a single large candle that was on top of a garden flower pot holder bought at a garage sale and she touched her flame to the wick. The flame was home. The flickering light rose from the candle with Olympic majesty, so long as Bruce cupped his hands around it to keep it from going out.

At the base of the pot holder was a security fence made from the netting of an onion bag. No vampires would douse the flame.

"Say, 'Let the games begin," Barb whispered to Kate.

"Let the games—" Kate started to say but before she could finish someone else yelled: "Car. Car."

A minivan pulled up. It stopped. The driver rolled down her window. "This is so cute, what are you doing?"

This is where Security would come in if there was Security.

"Having our own Olympics," said Barb, who was sort of the John Furlong of the events.

"You are not violating any Olympic rules, are you?" asked the driver of the minivan.

We do not know if that was a joke, or not. Olympia Pizza on Denman Street did not laugh when the Olympics committee ordered them to change their name. And it was even less of a joke when Olympia Pizza said "No!"

And it was no joke when there was no Olympia Pizza served at any Olympic venues. Of course, on the other hand Olympia Pizza became a hero in many eyes.

But on the street with the games, suddenly, the minivan and the mini-minded driver had changed the mood. The Olympic participants on the other side of the street heard none of this.

"No, we are fine," said Barb. The van drove off.

We will not get upset about a possible joke made about our street games. We will not. We will not let it affect our lives. We will not get annoyed. Okay, I am a little ticked off that the driver didn't say "That's cool, that's wonderful, what a neat idea." Instead the first words out of the mouth were a warning, funny or not.

It is amazing how fragile our lives are, how instantly joy can turn into a stiff back and cold water on the spirit. But we will not go along with the negative. "We are fine," Barb said. And then the van and the vibes passed, like most things.

Lesson: Keep your cool, always, and hang in there, always. That works. Always.

"Let the games begin," said Kate, again.

First up was wheelbarrow luging. Put a kid in a wheelbarrow and get a father to push it.

"Ready, get set…" Bruce, who is also a high school P.E. teacher, started off at Get Set.

"Wait. I didn't say 'Go' yet," said the starter.

"Next time," shouted Bruce who was rounding the first corner.

Jim Rennie and Perry Battista took off after him, each with a child banging their hands on the sides of their wheelbarrows. "Doesn't matter, we'll beat him," shouted Perry, who plays hockey every week.

They rounded the sewer plate. There was screaming. The fans were jumping up and down. The racers were coming down the home stretch.

"I won," shouted Bruce.

"No, this is the Finish line," Perry shouted as he passed Bruce and went to the next crack in the street.

"You both get a medal," said Barb, who had a tray full of aluminum foil medals of tinted blue and green and pink.

There was human curling on dollies with the sweepers using street brooms. The skips had a hard time because they had to go over the bumps of a sewer, and when their rocks made of wood on wheels with a human on top neared the circles drawn in chalk at the end of the course gravity took over. This is where Ron Strometski voiced his opposition. Ron is retired and has white hair and is clearly too old to be an Olympic athlete, except on this street.

"I'm winning. I'm winning," he said as his dolly slowed in the centre of the chalk circle.

But the street is arched, higher in the middle than the sides and as his dolly slowed going forward it started sliding sideways into the curb. Ron was slipping out of the circle. "Stop. Stop. I'm losing. I'm losing. Not fair," he shouted.

Gravity pulled him out of a first-place finish to the side of the street and bumped him against the curb.

"Do over," he shouted.

"We don't have do-overs in the Olympics," someone shouted.

"But I was going for gold," Ron said. "Now I've got the curb."

There was also two-man luging, which consisted of one man on the bottom on a dolly and one woman on top of the man, which technically does not qualify. It sounded nice in theory, but it did not work the way a man would hope and the race was cancelled because of technical problems. They tried it with the men lying face down, but neither man could hold his face and feet up enough to move forward. So they switched and the men were staring up at the sky. Then the women, both wives, climbed on top.

It was a family-rated game so the women tried to lay down also facing up. The balance was not as good as it was when they first met a few decades earlier. But it was the yelling from below about the discomfort from above that was the technical fault that eliminated the race from the record books.

Perry and Caroline did well in that event. Being younger might have had something to do with it. They held out longer than Bruce and Beth who rolled off the dolly before anyone could get them started. Perry and Caroline managed to get past the starting line but then they swung around and were going backwards down the street with Caroline shouting "Steer, steer," to Perry who could see nothing but the back of his wife's head.

In the end there were the medals made of aluminum foil over cardboard. The winners got to chose their colours and those awards will be cherished for the same amount of time as the medals that were given out in Whistler. The official medals will get more reverence, but the medals of the street have a better story.

But best were the bouquets, presented by Isobel and her friend, Amy, both of whom are thirteen. Isobel had spent the morning picking the only things growing in her backyard, which were weeds and leaves struggling in the February chill. Still, they were beautiful bouquets, just the right size for holding in a winner's hand, except the winners could only hold them for a minute or two because they had to be recycled for the next winners.

In the end everyone got a medal. Everyone got to hold a bouquet. Everyone owned the podium. Everyone went home happy. It was so easy, like the big games should be.

34

Sad is Also Memorable

It was a story I heard about when I was young, about the best athlete ever in the world. Every kid wants to hear about the best ever so they can grow up and be that too. Except with Jim Thorp the story was how mean people could be and how NOT to be like them.

A long time ago the Olympics were for amateurs. Professional athletes got paid to play, amateurs played for the pure love of sport, and the Olympics was for love. That's what they said. In truth, when that rule was made there were very few professional athletes in the world.

A fellow born on an Indian reserve in the western US was a very good runner, even though he could not afford running shoes, or any shoes. He also played football and baseball, better than just about anyone else, and everyone loved him because he was a nice, humble guy. His name was Jim Thorp. Some people say he was the greatest athlete ever in the entire history of the world, which would mean he was no slouch.

He went to a Native school and did a lot of running when he wasn't inside studying or working on his parents' small farm. When his school went to compete with other schools in track and field the coach would get off a train with Jim by his side and the coach of the other school would ask, "Where's your team?"

Jim's coach would look at Jim and say, "He's the team."

Then Jim's team with only Jim on it would win all the events.

In 1912 he went to the Olympics in Sweden. He won the biathlon and the triathlon. He was seven hundred points ahead of his nearest rival. He got gold medals in both. The king of Sweden said to him, "You, sir, are the finest athlete I have ever seen."

Jim Thorp replied, "Thanks, King." He knew how to handle a compliment.

As a gift, the king gave Jim a beautiful model of a Viking boat, which Jim could put on his dresser and place his gold medals inside.

But in America some people thought it was not good that a Native American should represent America and get such awards. Some people said the fastest feet in the world were nothing if they were not white. The people who did not like Jim because he was Indian searched through Jim's history and found what they hoped they would find.

For a baseball game that he was invited to play in away from home, he was once paid two dollars, which was used to pay for his room and board while he was there.

That, according to some, made him a professional athlete.

With glee, those who did not like him told the Olympic people that Jim Thorpe had lied about being an amateur and they had no choice but to take away his medals and send them back to Sweden. Even his Viking ship was taken away, even though it was a gift and not a medal.

Jim spent the rest of his life trying to make a living by playing for small-town baseball and football teams. There were no high-paying contracts then. He died broken and broke, just the way those who hated him wanted him to be. There's a lesson here.

If you are an ignorant, stupid bully you can ruin someone else's life. Of course you are still ignorant and stupid, but you probably don't know that.

Many years later, in the 1980s, Jim's elderly children got the Olympic committee to change its decision and they were awarded their father's medals. Actually, they were given duplicates because Jim's medals had been lost over the years. Where do you store returned Olympic medals?

During the Olympics in Vancouver, hockey players and skiers and skaters earned fortunes for winning. Advertisers lined up to give them money. That is why some athletes train so hard. Of course they do it also for the love and thrill of the sport, but money helps. One thing is for sure: if there is a podium in the sky Jim Thorp was sitting on it laughing when he heard the officials talking about the true spirit of the games.

Stories don't have to be all uplifting. Some can be downright sad, and revealing. That is life. And the story of Jim Thorp can make life more understandable.

One good thing: now in every sport where money and love and spirit are all plentiful, so is the mixture of colours and races of athletes. In the end, the bullies lost.

35

Protest Front Row

For everyone on earth, at least Canadians, Canada beating the US was the crowning moment of the Olympics.

I watched it with my neighbours and I was rooting for Canada. I know a good thing when I see it all around me.

But before the games began there was a shining gem of a moment.

There was an Olympic rally on the lawn outside the Art Gallery. Many people crowded around to hear the speeches and the hype and the music. Among them was Jazz, an eight-year-old, and her mother. Somewhere in the past their family was from India.

I watched the little girl cheering and beaming. I asked if she would like to be an Olympic athlete someday. I knew what the answer would be.

"Yes, so much."

"Do you like skiing or skating?"

She thought for a moment then said skating. That was nice. She looked like a delicate skater.

And then they came, from the back of the crowd pushing their way forward—protesters, youth, screaming, faces covered with bandanas, arms raised, pushing aside those who were there.

Jazz grabbed onto her mother who was trying to shelter her.

The protestors started shouting very bad words, the kind that Jazz's mother would not allow her daughter to say. They shouted in the faces of the people who were there. They jumped up and down and screamed and then one of them, a young man, jumped up on the stage and violently pushed aside the speaker, who was a woman.

He grabbed the microphone and screamed profanity into it, denouncing the Olympics as bad, bad, bad and even worse. It did not fit in with the world as he would like it.

The police were there before two blinks. They have a difficult job. They must control potential violence without stepping on the right of protest, which is supposed to be peaceful. The protesters did not wish to be peaceful. There was scuffling and handcuffing and lots of pictures taken by the protesters to demonstrate police brutality, which did not exist.

The crowd started singing "O Canada" while the protesters were screaming profanities.

I shook my head. I have seen protests that had meaning and strength and heart and soul. Soul, belief, was the real thing. It was what gave those protesters the strength and courage to continue. Those singing "O Canada" had soul.

I saw the civil rights protests with tens of thousands, hundreds of thousands, of people marching without their faces covered. They were silent, or they sang, one song: "We Shall Overcome". They were met by police with batons of hickory wood filled with lead. They were met by snarling dogs that were not kept under control. They were met by fire hoses powerful enough to break your ribs and legs. And they kept on marching.

And they were right. We all know that now. But a large part of the population did not know, or agree, when they were marching.

When I was in the US Air Force in the mid-1960s I was stationed at a base in northwest Florida, the sunshine state where everyone was happy going on vacation. Everyone except those who were not white. In the town next to the base where I was defending America there were separate drinking fountains for "coloured" people. And there was a separate entrance to the only movie in town, and inside they sat in the back of the balcony. And there was no toilet for them. They had to wait until the movie was over.

That was a reason to protest.

And now, a person who a short time ago could not drink from the same water fountain as a white person is leading that country. The protesters were right.

And I saw the anti-Vietnam war protestors, including veterans who had been there. They wore the same fatigues that they had worn when they were in the jungles of Vietnam. Tens of thousands, hundreds of thousands, marched on Washington, without violence.

Only a few times did things get out of hand, like at Kent State University when some college kids who were protesting the war were fired on by national guard troops. The national guard, unlike now, was made of part-time soldiers who rarely saw a rifle and never went to war. Over thirteen idiotic seconds they fired sixty-seven rounds at a group of unarmed students. Four were killed, nine wounded, one permanently paralyzed.

Four million students went on strike the next day, without violence.

I was reporting on some war veterans who took the Statue of Liberty hostage. I was on the outside of the door that they had chained shut from the inside.

"Why?" I asked.

"Because the war is wrong."

The were protesting for peace.

Eventually the war ended. It would not have, at least not then, according to Richard Nixon and Lyndon Johnson, had it not been for the protesters. In later decades most generals and nearly every politician who was involved in promoting the war said they were wrong.

The protesters were right.

And here today prior to the Olympic games was a group of violent, nasty, threatening youth who did not like money being spent on a sporting and cultural event, but most of all they did not like anything that most other people did like. That was their right. But it was not their right to frighten an eight-year-old who was singing "O Canada".

"Are you afraid?" I asked Jazz.

She held onto her mother's coat as a couple of bandana-covering-their-faces kids pushed past her trying to get to the stage.

"In other countries they would be thrown in jail and you would never see them again," said Jazz's mother. "They are so lucky they are here."

"Do you still want to be an Olympic skater?" I asked the little one.

"Yes," she said watching some of the protesters being handcuffed. "I want to win a medal for this country."

"And do the protesters scare you?" I asked again.

"A little," she said, "but they are just doing bad things. I want to do something good, so I won't be afraid."

Those were her words, exactly as they were on video tape. Again, eight years old.

Then Jazz and her mother left, squeezing through the crowd. They had made their statement.

They were right.

36

The Girl Who Would Not Say Santa

his is about a Grinch, who should have not been that. It is also about Rule Number Three. Any kid who gets in front of the camera, no matter how annoying, gets on television. The video version of that is no kid gets left on the cutting room floor. If a kid thinks he or she is going to be on TV and is home watching and he or she is not there, you have ruined a little world. The life equivalent is no kid should get ignored or pushed aside. Why would you hurt someone who is so small and hopeful?

This story happened during the Santa parade. I was at the end of the route, where I usually am, watching kids and their parents rushing to at least catch the final moment where the big guy is riding in the sleigh. We got that in the camera and we captured the kids being excited that Santa was coming and more excitement when he was there, right in front of them.

"Who's that?" I ask, knowing the answer but liking it when the faces brighten up and say: "That was SANTA!!"

159

Except for one little girl in a bright yellow coat.

"Who's that?" I asked.

She had a smile, but no words came out.

"Tell him it was Santa," her mother said.

The little girl said nothing.

"Tell him, tell him, or you'll never be on TV."

Her mother was almost shouting. She was angry. Her little girl was not performing as she should.

"Tell him it was Santa. Say it. Say Santa."

But the little girl said nothing. I suspect she was often told what to do and what to say. I could not say anything to the mother because I knew that might start an argument about who am I to tell her what to do with her child. But my heart was broken.

We went back to the TV station and in the dark edit room the whole story went together just as it was planned with the last little kid shouting the name Santa.

"Please put on the picture of the little girl who said nothing," I asked the editor.

"She didn't say anything," he said.

"Yes she did," I said. "You don't have to use words to say you've seen Santa. You can see it in her smile."

And that is what I said at the end of the story, with her face filling the screen. I hope her mother saw it. I hope her mother believes what she heard. And I hope her mother lets her see Santa in her own way.

P.S. Merry Christmas, little girl, and to your mother, who needs more Christmas.

Daffodils in January

"That can't be. That's impossible."

When I was young the only flowers I ever saw were at funerals. They were in vases and in wreaths. I had no idea why they were there or what you were supposed to do with them.

I grew up in a concrete world with concrete in front and concrete behind. No living thing was going to make it up through the ground. When we were in elementary school and read a Dick and Jane book there was a picture of Dick sitting by the side of a river with a piece of straw coming out of his mouth.

"What's a river, and where do you get straw?" we asked the teacher.

She shrugged. She was a city teacher in a school with concrete in the front and concrete in the back. The playground was concrete. "You get it in the country," she said.

"Where's that?"

"Far away."

Well, I have come far, to Vancouver where I now spend every spare minute in my backyard looking at flowers and pulling weeds and knowing I don't have to go any further to get to

161

heaven. And I know the purpose of flowers.

I also know that daffodils don't bloom in January. And peonies don't propagate in the winter. But there in a patch of Queen Elizabeth Park in mid-season of depression were reds and yellows and some blues. "Impossible."

For the impossible you stop. We got out just in time to see a woman quite far away pushing a wheelbarrow. For the impossible I will run.

"Hello, wait, stop."

The polite request worked. Or maybe it was the breathlessness.

"Did you plant those bits of spring into winter?"

She knew what I was talking about. "Yes, but don't tell anyone. I didn't want to throw them out."

Her name was Susan, she said, but then she said that's not her real name because she was not following her duties exactly rigidly. Her job was to take out the fading flowers from inside the Bloedel Conservatory and replace them with new, vibrant, potted hothouse blooms.

But on her way to the compost pile with the old flowers she made a detour, to here where I saw the beauty of spring, and there and over there where there were more out-of-season quirks. At each stop she took some freesias and crocuses but mostly hyacinths and daffodils and planted them. Then she slipped away.

If you were walking or driving on the south side of the park that day or for the rest of the week in January you would have seen bright yellow and blue and some pinks and whites. You would have seen the impossible.

I wanted to talk to her, but she said she had to go, she had to take her union-ordained and not-to-be-missed coffee break. She couldn't stay. We got three words out of her on camera. "I like them." And then she was gone.

Rule Two: Continuity is for wimps. In television, continuity means things should appear smoothly, without an eye-popping jump in the movement from item to item. It's really boring, but everything on television is seamless. You should not be able to see where the seams are connected. Of course, it's the seams that hold it all together.

In life, continuity means following the set procedure, the rules, so that everything gets done according to the book. That makes it easier for management, but again, it is boring.

Susan, which was not her name, broke with continuity. She broke the rules. Instead of going to the compost she turned her wheelbarrow to a bare patch of dirt and planted some fading flowers.

She messed up the order of her duties. Bless her.

Back to the straw between the teeth of Dick. We went to our friends in the corner bar because they were always there and available. They did not go to work. We did not know how they managed that. They would just stagger home at night. But they were grown up and they should know things that are important so we asked where we could get straw. They laughed at us and we didn't like being laughed at so we told them we would never go in their bar. We would stick with Coke.

Then we asked the man who ran the Jewish Deli, except we did not call it the Jewish Deli—it was just that all the delis were Jewish. The nice man behind the counter who sold me hot dogs every night for dinner after my mother came home from work still had numbers tattooed on his arm. His wife did also. We never talked about that.

All he would ever tell me each and every night when I would buy four hot dogs and a half pound of potato salad and one tomato was, "Don't vorry, Mickey, dings vill get better. They alvays do." And then he would give me a pickle to eat on my way home. I was never sad when I left there.

Where can we get straw, we asked?

"Vell, I don't know. Ve have no straw here. But you should use your imagination and dink ver der might be straw."

Then he smiled. I remember to this moment the smile and the hint. He left his spot behind the counter and took his broom and started sweeping the floor. "Dis is a goot broom," he said. "You know vat it is made of?"

He said nothing more. I ran out of the store and home with my hot dogs and before I got in my front door one kid came out of his apartment and said he was still looking for straw.

"Listen," I said. "The nice man in the deli told me a secret." And I told him.

I finished eating my hot dogs and ran back outside just as the kid I had told the most important thing in the world to was coming out of his door. He had half a dozen sticks of straw he had cut from his mother's broom. "She won't even notice it's gone," he said.

We sat up against a building on the concrete and wiped the strands of straw clean on our pants and stuck them in our mouths. Suddenly the concrete was gone. There was a river in front of us, we said, just like in the picture in the book. We were in the country and if anyone doubted it we could say we've got straw, and you can only get straw in the country so that's where we are.

Rule Two: Continuity is for wimps. No one puts straw from an old, used broom in their mouths, unless it is not from an old, used broom that you would not need to use because you are in the country where it grows everywhere.

The river was beautiful that day, and the straw was growing all around us.

38

Jack Benny Plays East Hastings

The discovery thrilled me. It was like finding gold, or a quarter on the ground, but this was better because this I could give away without having less of it, and that made it more valuable than anything.

"You remember Jack Benny and Mary Livingstone?" I asked a pair of women of age and dignity. They had just come out of the new Woodward's Food Floor.

Oh, my gosh. What did I just say? The new Woodward's Food Floor. There is so much in that name. It is like saying "Cool Cat," or "Submarine Race Watching." Okay, you don't know what I am talking about.

Submarine race watching is what you did with a girl when it was dark and you were alone and you were a cool cat. There were no submarines involved, or cats. But for many of us our thoughts never went deeper than wondering how you could watch submarines racing.

You get the picture. Words, especially old forgotten ones, are the wall switches for warm memories.

Woodward's Food Floor lights up an era, a time and space, when Hastings Street was suave and safe and *the* place to be. Everyone went to Woodward's, and the main part of your groceries, including the food you could not get anywhere else, like Marks and Spencer's meat pies, you could get at the Woodward's Food Floor.

And then you walked down the street with your mother and she bought a dress and said hello to other mothers who had come to buy meat pies and Scottish bacon that had both the side and end pieces together in one slice so that it looked like a strip with a round piece at the end. Hastings Street, both east and west, was where everything was. After that you took the streetcar home. I have written about this before. East Hastings was thriving. The first city hall was at the corner of Main and Hastings. The soldiers marched along the street before going off to be killed while protecting it.

That was the era when Benjamin Kubelsky was telling jokes on stage at the Pantages Theatre on East Hastings. He travelled in the burlesque circuit around the US and Canada.

Being away from home, he would take any invitations to home-cooked meals he could get. One of them was from a friend of a friend to a special holiday dinner at the home of David Marks, a Vancouver tailor. It was a Passover Seder in an apartment building on East Hastings at the corner of Jackson Street. It was a traditional dinner with the bitter herbs representing the slavery in which the Jews were held in Egypt and the sweet sauce representing their freedom. But while the prayers were said and the stories were told, Benny saw Sadie at the table. She was fourteen. He was twenty-four. She was much, much too young for him. He was much, much too old.

Nothing would ever come of this, for sure.

But he fell in love. Or she did. It depends on who told the story. But whoever it was, Benjamin Kubelsky kept coming back to Vancouver to perform at the Pantages and he would walk down the street to knock on Sadie's door. He did this for six years. Eventually she was old enough, and he asked her and she said yes, and Sadie became Mrs. Kubelsky.

Then Benny Kubelsky changed his name to Jack Benny. And soon Sadie joined his act as Mary Livingstone.

In time they became one of the most famous comic couples in North America, along with George Burns and Gracie Allen. And then, in time, after their deaths their reruns faded from the airwaves and you had to be of a certain mature age to know of them.

During the same decades that the popularity of their humour was dying, the same thing was happening to the street that they walked on holding hands. Because of many things, but mostly drugs, East Hastings went from The Place To Be to The Place To Avoid. Woodward's closed and the Pantages Theatre was boarded up, along with almost everything else on the street.

Skip ahead several decades and through the miracle of determination and some creative business deals East Hastings is coming back. Woodward's department store has been replaced by the beautiful Woodward's condo and social housing structure. And yes, it is beautiful. It has coloured strips of wrought iron on the outside over a burnished red exterior. The architecture was copied from the Hotel Europe, about ten blocks away in Gastown.

This is a wandering story, forgive me, but all stories, all relationships, all events wander until they find they are connected, somehow.

The Hotel Europe was built by Angelo Calori, an inspired architect who believed the small city of Vancouver would grow into a metropolis. He put his life savings into creating the first reinforced concrete building in Canada. It was also the first fire-proof hotel in Western Canada. We can sleep here and not burn to death—there was a novel concept.

And he built it on a lot where it was impossible to build anything. It was triangular. You can't make a triangular building, he was told. Buildings have four sides, not three.

He made it with three sides. And it was beautiful and it was in Gastown, which was thriving.

Angelo Calori with his derby and walking stick was so proud. He stood in front of the building to allow someone to indulge himself and his hotel with a new invention called photography.

His hotel was six stories high with a beer parlour on the ground floor. He knew it would be a success. It was in the centre of the new city.

The hotel was finished in 1909. By 1910 Vancouver was moving west. First the giant Dominion Trust Building went up at Hastings and Cambie, the tallest building in the British Commonwealth. Two years later the World Tower rose a few blocks away, replacing the Dominion Building as the tallest in the Commonwealth.

They were the towering, twenty-storey structures that drew other builders and beer parlours and visitors and hotel guests to the west, away from Calori's hotel. He went bankrupt, but his hotel stayed and is still a work of art.

And if you drive along Powell Street toward the Woodward's building and look at it, and then a few blocks later you swing over to Water Street and look at the Hotel Europe you say, "That's the same building." You say it even if there's no one to say it to. The new Woodward's building is a copy of the Hotel Europe, just a bit larger, and it is in the new centre of the city.

Calori would be proud. It just took a while.

"Of course we know them," said one of the women of age

outside Woodward's Food Floor, which is not owned by Woodward's. The grocery store is now run by a company called Nesters, which deals in high-class foods and was not born until after Woodward's died.

"It's not the same as the old Woodward's Food Floor," many say.

No. But then Woodward's isn't either. And this street that had gone from the top of the ladder to the bottom rung, and even lower—in fact the ladder had sunk into the mud—is now coming back. And it is not the same, thankfully. And Woodward's Food Floor along with a hundred other things is helping bring it up.

And yes, we are now back at the beginning with the ladies outside the food floor whom I was asking about Jack Benny and Mary Livingstone. Stories that go in a straight line are easy to follow, but they are not like life, which is a road with many exits and entrances and side trips.

"Yes, of course, we used to listen to them on the radio, back when the real food floor was here," said the ladies.

"But do you know where Mary Livingstone came from?" I love asking questions like that because it is so good to see the surprise on their faces when they hear the answer. In one moment, right after they say "No" I'll point and say, "She came from right down this street." They will say, "Noooo??? Really??" And I'll feel good.

"She came from Vancouver," they said. "Everyone knows that."

What?!! How did they know? Look at my face for the surprise. I just learned it yesterday when I read the plaque on the building at Hastings and Jackson. I was doing a story about a woman's drop-in centre across the street when I turned around and saw the old brass plate on the front of an ancient apartment house.

They knew because that was big celebrity news during the 1950s. Who in Vancouver would not know that one of the most famous and funny women in the world came from Vancouver? But I was not here in the 1950s.

To know this, I needed to see a plaque which said that Sadie Marks lived here in 1919 when she was fourteen and met Benjamin Kubelsky. It told briefly of their lives, and condensed into three lines a great love affair and marriage that lasted forty-seven years and ended only when death did them part.

But it didn't matter. I was thrilled that I was standing outside the door where Sadie held hands with Benny after their dates, when this was a high-class neighbourhood. Now the U-2 corner grocery takes up the first floor of the building, and across the street are women selling their services for twenty minutes to buy a half-hour of chemical highs. But back in the dating days of Sadie and Benny this was a number one neighbourhood. Sadie and Benny would have carried home pickles and bread from Woodward's, and then said goodnight, with a kiss on the cheek.

Yes, on the cheek. Can you imagine that now? That alone is worth ten minutes of thought. She was young and that was a different era. I am sure the kiss slid more central over time, but not at first. She was a good Jewish girl and this was a good Christian age. The cheek was a start.

But now that I knew what happened here I couldn't wait to tell someone. The only problem was the first two ladies I met already knew. Darn. There goes my story.

But of course, the surprise that they knew makes the story better.

39

The Football Player

If I want inspiration I go to East Hastings. Three years ago I humbly predicted that someday folks would take a tour of Vancouver and when the bus got to Main and Hastings the driver would announce, "Welcome to the trendiest part of town."

It is coming. It is getting closer. Today, but it could have been any day, I saw a guy sweeping the sidewalk on the corner of Carrall and Cordova. That is a block from Pigeon Park. That is fifty steps from what was one of the most disgusting drug dealing corners in the city.

Now there are fancy restaurants in Blood Alley, half a block from where he was sweeping. There is a bar with upscale patrons sitting at a window right behind where he was sweeping. Pigeon Park has been redesigned to make it less a hangout space and so there are fewer folks hanging out there.

But what made me stop and talk to the guy sweeping was the football on the sidewalk near where his broom was working.

"Hi," I said. That is a good way to begin. "Do you work here a lot?"

"Every day," he said.

"Are you getting paid for this?"

"No, but sometimes someone will come out of one of the shops and give me something."

He had tattoos up each arm, homemade tattoos, the kind you do yourself if you have nothing else to do. The kind of tattoos that are done with a sewing needle or a piece of broken glass and a bottle of ink. They are not artsy, they are rough.

"Mind telling me what you do with the football?"

"I just kick it," he said. "It is kind of my medicine ball."

He had a cigarette behind his ear and his body was lean and wiry, but he spoke so well. It was as though he had lots of time to read and formulate things.

"Did you play football, I mean for a professional team, or something like that?" I was hoping that he would say he was a former BC Lions player or something, anything, to give him a reason for having a football with him because that would give the story life. I can't stand the answer "I just like it," or "I have it for the exercise." Boring.

"I played when I was in the pen."

"What did you say?"

"I played when I was behind bars, just for something to do."

Okay, he wins. Anything you learn in prison besides how to go back to prison is a bonus.

"How long?"

"Seventeen years. But not all at once," he said. Even someone who has spent almost half his adult life in prison does not want you to think he is all bad.

"I was there three times, for forgery, to feed my heroin habit. That was back in the days when you got real sentences."

This guy had been around. And he was honest, which is something you seldom find behind bars or in front of them.

He said he kicked a football around the prison yard day after day and it had become his medicine ball, his contemplation, his peace maker. "It's good for soothing the day. And I don't have a dog or a cat so this is my friend."

There is a side note in here. Have you ever kicked a football? It doesn't go where you think it will. You cannot play football alone. You can throw a tennis ball against a wall and catch it, alone. You can toss a basketball into a hoop and catch it, alone. You cannot play football alone. And if you try, it takes patience.

The man with the patience was Mike Haggerty. Age: forty-nine. Life experience: one hundred plus. Problem: "Sometimes my ball is stolen. When I am not looking, when I'm sweeping the street, someone scoops up the ball and puts it under his jacket and I look around and can't tell who it is."

And there is the irony. The guy who has spent many years locked up for breaking the law big time is ticked off at someone for breaking the law small time. But it really doesn't make any difference whether it is big or small. When something bad is done to you by someone else, even if it is just stealing a football, it hurts. That's the only word to describe it. The extent of the hurt is just a measurement compared to others, but always your hurt is the worst.

Did I say "just" stealing a football? Am I an idiot? There is no little crime. You have your newspaper stolen and you feel rotten. You have a million dollars swindled or have your car stolen or your credit card when you turn around to get a cup of coffee, and you are hurt.

Mike was hurt that someone would steal his football.

"It's like taking my tools. It's part of me," he said.

I asked what advice he would give to anyone who was thinking of stealing his football.

"Get a job," he said. "Any job, even if it pays nothing, like mine. And stop hurting others. It's not nice."

I looked around. Skid row was becoming less and less skid-dish. Where there were abandoned stores a year ago now were coffee shops, fancy ones like Waves that opened two stores—one at Cordova and Main and one at Pender and Main. I talked to the owner of the shops.

"We expect the neighbourhood will go up, quickly. People with jobs buy lattes," he said.

To the west, where East Hastings becomes West Hastings, a new Bean Around The World opened in a beautiful, historic white-painted building. It is at the corner of Hastings and Cam-bie. Eight years ago I did a story about the last business, a men's clothing store, to close in that building. The owner said all his customers had gone. "Look out my window," he said. "There's nothing but crime and drugs out there, no business in here."

Today, lattes are sipped on that same street.

It is getting better.

What were once boarded-up flop houses are now revitalized, government-financed, low-income rooming houses. Where there were needles on the ground is now clean pavement, because of anti-poverty agencies that hire people to pick up garbage, and because of Mike.

I have done stories about people who are moving into the area, along Cordova and Carrall. I admired them. They have courage and can see the future and they are making a part of that future a part of right now. But most shocking to me was when the Web Master at Global TV said he was moving into a condo behind Number Five Orange.

"What!!"

You have to have the picture in mind. Peter Meiszner is a slightly built young guy who is a genius with computers and web-sites. He designs and posts what you read about the news and blogs and stuff like that. But he looks like a trendy Yale Towner,

174

the kind who would have one glass of white wine with his friends while they talked about the excitement of going out to a club at night. I don't know if he does that, but he looks like it. If he stood on a scale I don't think it would register.

"Why did you move behind the Number Five? And also aren't you afraid?"

"It's not as bad as you think. In fact, at night it is quieter than downtown."

"Are you going to stay?"

"It's my neighbourhood."

Peter, and people like him, are making that neighbourhood theirs, sharing it, elevating it, just by living in it. Because of him and others like him, "Welcome to Fabulous Main and Hastings" is coming sooner than even I believed.

And back at Carrall and Cordova where there once was a guy with no future now there was someone standing under a football coming down into his hands. A rule in football is you can always turn around the game and win, no matter how far behind you are. Always. You just have to keep moving the ball, you have to keep the other side from stealing it, and don't rest until the ball is over the line. When we left Mike he had his ball resting on the sidewalk next to one of the expansion lines in the concrete while he was sweeping.

In his next move he picked up his cardboard and swept up the dirt. Then he moved the ball with him, over the line. The game would be long, and he had a lot of cleaning up to do, but in the end he would win. I know, because he said he would.

40

The Doubter

"**Y**ou don't really believe all this, do you? I mean all this stuff about positive thinking."

"Well, yes."

"But suppose you get a very late cameraman, and he is miserable because he's already done two stories, and it is raining and then you get an editor who is not happy because he's done three stories. You can't tell me you are going to have a good day."

That is Karen Deeney, the chief editor. She figures out how the show will actually make it to air. And that is not just one show. She has to pair up editors with reporters for the noon show, the five o'clock show and the six. That is an impossible task since some of the editors will not work with some of the reporters. And some reporters will not work with some editors, although no one will admit that.

Of course anyone will work with anyone when it comes to the crunch, but in reality some people get along with certain people better than some other people. Look at your family. You may be thinking that one person in it is crazy.

It is similar with editors as seen from the inside of a human brain (mine), which sees things any way it wants: the editors in Karen's charge are crazy. All TV editors are. They work in small rooms with no windows and a bank of monitors in front of them. They have to deal with reporters and producers who slip into their rooms, sit beside them, and panic.

176

They never see daylight. Some have spent thirty years in the dark rooms and have never known what the weather is outside. And then they get a producer pulling open the door to their room, skipping the "Hello, how are you?" part and starting with, "I need a picture of the prime minister saying the world is coming to an end. And I need it NOW."

The editor has listened to the speech from Ottawa. There is no such comment from the chief of all chiefs.

"But he must have said it. I heard someone say he said it."

Actually an assistant to the prime minister said that the speech at the end of the meeting would be coming to the world soon.

"Oh," says the producer, and leaves, without a goodbye or a thank you.

Editors keep the world, and news, honest. But they are not appreciated, and that can drive you crazy.

"Suppose you get one of them in a bad mood?" Karen asked.

Karen likes to tell me she is not a Pollyanna. "I do not believe that everything turns out happy."

But she does. I know, because I watch her. She was a field producer for CNN in war zones. She met her soulmate while he was in the Canadian army in Bosnia and she was covering the war. Impossible situations are just part of her daily tea.

"We have three reporters coming in by four," a producer tells Karen. "All their stories are needed by five."

Impossible.

"We'll try to get it done," says Karen.

"There is a shooting downtown and we need live coverage." One live truck is in Surrey, one is in Abbotsford and the other has a flat tire.

Impossible.

But, "We'll try to get it done."

"We have three stories that will be late for six." One is from

Afghanistan, one from London, one from New Orleans. "And we expect some trouble with the satellite link."

Totally impossible.

But,…and you know the rest.

"We will have to see if a couple of editors can do a couple of extra stories in a little less time," says Karen with just a hint of mock horror.

I don't know how she does it. Actually the editors do it. But the editors would not organize it and slip in extra stories and then do an extra story, and one more after that, all of which are mentally exhausting, unless Karen encouraged them to do it. They do the impossible, every day.

"But I don't believe in that Pollyanna stuff that everything works out just because you believe it will," she reminds me.

No. She's right. She doesn't have to admit it. And I agree. That Pollyanna stuff is for those who can't get the job done and just pretend. The real positive thinkers don't have to talk about it.

41

Pin Setters

I look at video games and sigh. You get all the excitement a robot needs from pushing your thumb, very quickly. The thumbs pound, the eyes stare and the excitement is in the hand and the head. The trouble is the adrenalin doesn't pump.

Phooey.

Let me take you to a game very few have played. It was like swimming in the cardboard boxes, but more dangerous. Swimming in cardboard is in book number two, *Back Alley Reporter*. That was when the kids in my neighbourhood would climb onto the roof of a factory and dive into the boxes that were piled up behind a fence two stories high.

We swam all day. We chased each other under the big, uncrushed boxes, which to us was the same as being under the water and that was good because we did not have any water to swim in. And when kids from another street wanted to take control of our boxes away from us we fought with fists and feet on the sidewalk to hold onto our brown ocean. But that story has already been told. Get the book. I guarantee you will get some boxes of your own to swim in.

But this other sport we got paid for. I remembered it when I went into the Grandview bowling lanes on Commercial Drive in Vancouver. That is my favourite bowling alley in the world because it is a family-owned business on a family-friendly street.

On a wall over the Coke machine is a large black and white

179

picture of Louis Marino, formal and stern in a suit jacket and tie. He needed a way to support his family. It was 1947. He was an immigrant. The war had just ended. He thought people might want to have some fun so he opened a bowling alley on one of the city's busy, but not high-class, streets.

Three generations later the Marinos are still running the place. Tammy Marino is mostly in charge. She's in her twenties, cute as a bunny rabbit and tough as a mongoose, just like a bowling alley chick should be. She knows almost everyone who comes in. She knows their shoe size. Sometime her parents drop by, sometimes her grandmother comes in. They are in charge on paper, but Tammy runs the place.

That is the way a family business works. You grow up in the business and stay there. But there was something she didn't know.

I wander in looking for a story. In that same alley I met Sid the nearly blind 101-year-old bowler who played a game shortly before he died. And I watched my granddaughter rolling balls in the psychedelic alley upstairs on her fourth birthday. There are no age limits on bowling.

"I got to show you this. I had only heard about this, I didn't know about it," said Tammy. "We're renovating. We're putting in some ten-pin lanes and you got to see what we found."

Most of Grandview Lanes has five-pin lanes. In case you did not know, five-pin bowling is played only in Canada. It was invented in Ontario in 1909 by Thomas Ryan to make the game more a thinking contest. With a small ball you could pick and choose your pins instead of rolling a ten-pin ball that looks like it came out of a cannon that is simply on a mission to destroy.

In the Canadian game the pins are worth different values, the centre one is five points, the two behind it three each and the outer two in the back two points each. It is not quite like chess, but you can work on scoring more points than in ten-pin, in which all the pins are worth the same and the object is quantity destruction.

"Come, follow me," said Tammy. She walked between two lanes to the back where the pin-setting machines were grinding and bumping.

"Duck under here."

She held her hand so I would not bang my head. I scooted under the boards and stood up in a world of mechanical arms and pulleys and the banging noise of one of the world's greatest inventions: the automatic pin setter.

Suddenly I was sixteen again, but before I could finish the feeling Tammy said, "Look," and she pointed at the wall over the machines.

There, drawn on the plywood, uncovered when they ripped away some plasterboard, were the pin setters of the 1950s and '60s. They were half life-sized. They were fantastic.

They were beatniks, they were bohemians, they were renegade misfits of society who had made a living and found a life in the back of a bowling alley. One of them was an artist, probably most of them were artists, but one of them had a dark, broad pencil and drew a gallery of his fellow inhabitants in a place where the pins went flying and the jokes were loud and raunchy and the concussions occasional.

Some had goatees, some wore caps, all had the long, defiant hair of the early '60s, but not the shoulder length of the hippies of the '70s. By then hair was a statement. You advertised your political, social and moral beliefs by the length of your hair. But that was started by the beatniks, who were radical if they skipped two weeks between haircuts.

There were pictures of a half-dozen guys and girls, all of whom shared the nasty life at the end of the alley. I did not know their names. But I knew them better than their names because I had been one of them.

In the late 1950s I set pins at a ten-pin lane in New York. It was the kind of job you could get by walking into the alley and saying you wanted to work. The only question was, "Kid, are you sure you want to do this?"

We could not afford to play so we made a game out of back of the lanes. Plus we got paid for it.

You got fifty cents a game plus tips. The tips could be nothing, the danger was high and the night seemed like it would never end. What more could you hope for as you tried to make enough money to buy beer and cigarettes, which was the goal of every sixteen-year-old if we could find someone to buy the beer for us, which was not likely.

Ten-pin was more than twice as hard as five-pin. The pins were bigger and had no rubber wrapped around their middle like the five-pins. When they got hit hard they took off and you would sit on a thin strip of wood between the lanes with your arms covering your head. That left your ribs exposed and when a pin hit you there it would hurt like a two-by-four banging into your side. But it was better than getting hit in the head.

Then you would jump down and scoop away the pins that were left lying on the alley and send the ball rolling in a return track back to the bowler. After he threw the second ball you would grab the ball and send it back again. That gave you about twenty seconds to grab a pin in each hand and use your foot to push down on a metal bar that would raise up steel pins in the floor of the alley. The wooden pins each had a hole in the bottom. You would put the wooden pins over the steel spikes and keep doing this until all ten pins were standing up.

The game was to get it done before the other pin setters at the back of their alleys. The game was also to stay alive because just when you finished setting up the pins the bowler in the next lane was starting to throw the ball. You jumped back on the wooden strip and held your head. Every pin boy had two lanes to take care of. So the ball in the other lane would be smashing down the pins as you cowered. Then you would jump down and scoop away wayward pins while the ball in the first lane was crashing into its pins.

You would jump over to that lane and scoop away pins at about the time that the ball in the other lane was coming back at full speed. It was like a video game in which you were ducking from the zaps.

Somewhere in this world of banging and flying hunks of wood you would get a chance to shout to Joey, who was two lanes away.

"How you doin'?"

Bang.

"Faster than you," he would say.

Bang, crash.

"What about you?" Tommy.

"Faster than you."

Then from two lanes down, ugh, crash, thud, "Owww."

"Sounds like Tommy. He didn't duck," said Joey.

Bang again.

But the real challenge came when two bowlers in your adjoining lanes who had been drinking lots of beer took long drags on their cigarettes, then both of them threw their balls together. You could see the balls coming. There was no escape. You got on your strip of wood and squeezed down as tightly as you could and covered your head.

Bang, Bang. The pins came flying from both sides and you could only stay down until they stopped bouncing off the walls and off your ribs.

"You still alive?" asked Joey.

"I'm going to need a beer. Do you know anyone who will buy it for us?"

But before the beer you had to get two lanes, up to twenty pins, set up at once. Impossible.

"Hey, kid. No tip for you. You're too slow," the bowlers shouted from the other end of the lanes. Then they would laugh.

Now compare that with a video game. I know. You'd have to be crazy not to pick the video. But when I looked at the drawings on the wall at the end of the allies over the automatic pin setters in Grandview Lanes, I knew them. I understood them. Even if they were five-pin folks, I was still proud to have been in their company.

"That was before my time," said Tammy. "But my grand-mother used to set pins back here, and they said she could do six lanes at one time."

Granny, you are my hero. Back in my old neighbourhood you would have won every game.

Luizs and the Boxes

I am lucky, because often when I go to work I do not go to work.

Sometimes a week goes by and I don't set foot inside the studio. I meet camera folks outside, find the stories, then edit and write in one of the mobile microwave or satellite trucks. Then I go home. That is a nice way to live.

But I do miss seeing Luizs. She is the only Louise in the world who spells her name Luizs. I know this because she made up the name herself, and you have to like her for that.

She looks sort of like Dolly Parton, except she is a hundred pounds lighter and five inches shorter but still has the same dimensions. She has puffy blonde hair and bright red lipstick and a beautiful smile, except when someone is on the phone complaining about the way we do news or the way the world is run or moaning about their sad lives.

"Sir, you really should take care of your problems yourself instead of calling a television station."

"No, we just report the weather, we do not control it no matter what you believe."

"No, I have checked everywhere and we did not do a story

185

about the government giving everyone in the country a $1,000 bonus… No, this is not CBC… No, this is Global… Oh, you made a mistake. Goodbye, and good luck."

The phone is replaced in its holder. Then Luizs bangs her head on the desk, ever so gently. She does not want to mess up her hair.

"Ten minutes I spent looking for that story. Ten minutes while everyone else was on hold. Ten minutes and he called the wrong station.

"But I still love them."

Luizs answers the phones in the newsroom. Every reporter, every cameraman, every anchor and every member of the public who calls the newsroom goes through Luizs. It is an impossible job. And she knows everyone who calls and says to her, "It's me." She knows who "me" is.

She can also fix the photocopier, which makes her truly invaluable.

But what she did for me was above the call of love or duty.

I asked her if she had any small boxes. My wife uses them to teach kids how to build things. Any small box will do. They come in different shapes and sizes and colours, perfect for helping little minds learn to think outside of big boxes.

"I will look around," said Luizs.

Many people have said that when I've asked. Most mean to do it, but most, as is the human condition, forget.

The next day she had some boxes. In fact, she had many boxes. She had a large box filled with little boxes that had once held paper clips and staples and pens and notebooks and tape.

"Where did you get so many boxes?" I asked.

"Shhhhh," she said, and opened a draw in the office supply desk. It was filled with paperclips and staples and pens.

"But you can't do that," I said.

"And why not? Your wife needs boxes, here are the boxes."

"But what about people who need paper clips?"

"They are still here, just in a little more old-fashioned way. You have to put your hand in and take out what you need instead of grabbing a whole box."

"And what about the staples?"

"Does your wife need the boxes?"

"Yes. But I can't ask you to dump out all the staples."

"You're not asking. Here's the boxes."

Luizs doesn't have to be asked to do things.

The next day I went into the station again.

"Luizs has a present for you."

I worried. Presents scare me.

It was a large silver-coloured cardboard box, beautiful.

"Open it," said Luizs.

A small crowd gathered. It did not matter to them why I was getting a present, they just wanted to know what the present was. That is a strange thing with the human condition. We want to see what is under the wrapping even more than having it. The surprise of one new thing beats ten old things hands down. That's what keeps the consumer society going.

Just as an aside, you know there has been nothing new in soap powder or soap bars or dish soap or body soap for a hundred years. It is still made the same way, basically squeezing some kind of fat together which will carry away dirt when it gets wet.

Check an earlier story, no fair skipping them, because it is close to impossible to find a bottle, bar or box of soap in a supermarket that does not say NEW on it. Sometimes NEW AND IMPROVED. I once read in a marketing manual that no cleaning product should ever be sold without the word NEW on the label no matter how old it is. Otherwise, it will not sell.

"What's in Luizs' present? What's new? Open it."

I opened the box and it was filled with paper clip boxes and staple boxes and more pen boxes and note pad boxes.

Luizs had gone around the entire building and emptied every box of staples and paper clips and pens in Global BC. For the next year at least, maybe more, anyone needing staples or pens or clips will open a drawer and find piles of them, without boxes. They will find them the way they were in the days of the general store, just pens and clips, no boxes. It will look odd.

Some will say, "Hey, how come these are all just piled in the drawer? How come there's no boxes?"

And someone else will say, "Luizs needed boxes."

And the reply will be, "Oh." And no one will question it because they know whatever Luizs wants she will get, regardless of whether it is in the desk of the president or the utility supply cabinet downstairs.

She made the day good for me. She gave me what I wanted. But more than that, every day she gives herself whatever she wants. She is never sick, never angry, never frustrated. She has made her life the way she wants it. That is amazing. It is like fishing with a string and a stick and knowing you will catch a fish. You need boxes, you get boxes, simple.

She is also in the lowest category of the union salary scale. She should be in the highest. The contract should have a category for stealing boxes. She would be at the senior level.

43

You Believe in the Impossible, Don't You?

One other story about Luizs.

I had known Luizs for twenty years when one day she said, "Don't you think you could spell my name right?"

I know she said that right after she said, "You dummy." But she was sweet enough not to say that part out loud.

But seriously, have you ever heard of anyone, ANYONE, anywhere in the world who spells Luizs like Luizs spells Luizs?

She wanted something different, she said, so she invented the spelling herself. I checked. As far as I can find out she is the only Luizs on the planet.

For that alone, she is special.

But she also has that magic stuff.

"I can't find a story again," I said when I called her.

"Not again," she said.

"Yes, again," I said.

You see, our conversations are deep.

"Okay, I'll cross them," she said.

When she crosses her fingers I find a story. That's how it works. But Luizs was having a problem. I had asked her too many times to cross them and her fingers were getting tired. It is hard to answer phones and transfer calls when your fingers are crossed.

"I'm slipping," she said. "My fingers are slipping."

Sweat was building between her index and her middle finger. If she uncrossed them the magic would be gone. She knew that and she was struggling.

"What's wrong?" Brian Coxford asked her.

"McCardell needs help again," she said. "But my fingers can't hold on."

Brian, who is one of the best reporters in the world, always has a way of getting right to the heart of the matter. He grabbed some Scotch tape and wrapped it around Luizs' two fingers. Saved. Her fingers stayed together and presto, halfway across town, we found a group of young girls hired by the PNE to shovel sawdust into the barns, and none of them had ever done any hard work in their lives. Perfect story. And all thanks to Luizs and Brian and Scotch tape.

Maybe they should teach the theory of the crossed fingers in journalism school. If you know something is telling you that you will find a story you have to find it, and there is no possible way it will not happen. Scotch tape helps.

As for the spelling of her name: you can't teach imagination like that anywhere. It's not like magic, it is magic.

44

I'm an Old Man, At Last

"You f***ing, stupid old man."

Amazing. I had never been called that before.

The young guy in the new BMW had cut in front of my wife and me on the highway. He was a super driver because a car could not really fit into that tiny space. I jammed on my brakes to assist him in his racetrack career, and gave him a friendly little beep to let him know we were still alive. That was while the adrenalin was draining out of my heart.

I knew the young fellow was very good at squeezing into those spaces because a minute later I saw him slip into a tiny opening in front of a minivan filled with children. When they beeped he acknowledged it by waving his longest finger at the children. Then he drove across three lanes of traffic and went back to the van to wave some more. He was a very accomplished driver, doing all that with one hand on the wheel and looking out the side window.

Shortly after that he slowed until he was in front of my wife and me again after squeezing in and greeting us with the same finger. It looked like a very well-exercised finger.

Then he went into the lane alongside us, rolled down his

window and, while still waving, he spat at us. I admired his driving skills even more: one hand on the wheel and no eyes on the road. This was one unusually experienced motorist.

It was then he called me a "f***ing, stupid old man."

I had heard the first word before. It comes from those with limited speaking ability, reduced by even more limited brain size. As for calling me "stupid," well, I keep trying to learn things. Be patient.

But never before in my life have I been called an "old man." It was the first time. I felt so grown up, so mature, so distinguished. Old men know things that young people who wave fingers don't know. Old men don't get upset. Old men know that people who push themselves into tight spaces and spit eventually run into a brick wall, or someone with a brick in their hand who will not like being cut off.

Old men know that finger-waving young men who show off their driving skills usually don't become old men.

That is good enough to know.

45

Shopping Together

Lisa Valancius of East Vancouver wrote to me that her mother had died recently and she was very sad. But her mother had been a wonderful woman who celebrated Halloween to the highest level. She decorated her house inside and out and invited everyone to come and enjoy it.

To remember her mother, Lisa decorated the house again and invited everyone to come and celebrate her life on Halloween evening, scaring each other and giving out candy.

When I read that, I knew Lisa is the daughter every mother would want, and her mother was the mom everyone would love to have.

It reminded me of my mother's death and the funeral my kids and I gave her. I've told this story before, but it always makes me feel good.

My mother lived alone in a tiny apartment in New York. Her passion was shopping, even though she could not afford to buy much. She would hunt through racks and shelves until she found something she liked, a blouse or belt, basically anything. But she would not buy it. She would go back to the store over and over waiting for it to go on sale. If she got lucky, she went home with something special at half price. If she missed it, there was always the next store and the next blouse. She never had more than two or three blouses in her closet.

Before she died she left a note saying she did not believe in any religion and to dispose of her remains any way we thought efficient.

We thought, "Yes."

My daughter made a list of all the high-end department stores in New York: Lord and Taylor, Saks Fifth Avenue, Bonwit Teller…you get the idea, fancy places. Then we took the ashes of the woman who was a mother and a grandmother and we secretly carried them into the stores. When no one was watching we sprinkled Grandmother in front of the racks filled with blouses and the glass counters with belts and other nice things.

My son went into Tiffany's, the fanciest jewellery store in the world and one in which my mother would never have gone, and when the guards turned their heads he sprinkled Grandma in front of the diamonds.

We walked across the red carpet in front of The Plaza, one of the top of all top hotels, and sprinkled Grandma. Then we watched the shoes of the well heeled pick her up and carry her inside.

She is buried all over New York, and now she does not have to go to the blouses. They come to her.

Thanks, Lisa, for reminding me of that. Our mothers can go shopping together and then give out candy to the kids.

46

The Grubs and the Song

"My gosh, look at those lawns," I said to Tony Clark.

We are, as always, looking for something good, something uplifting, but I can't get my eyes off front lawns that look like tanks have crossed them and then used them for target practice.

"Want some pictures of them?" Tony asked.

Tony is the cameraman I was with when we did the story called "Getting To The Bubble," which became the title story of a book a few years ago. In brief, that was the tale of searching for more than half a day for something, anything, and time after time almost getting it. "Almost," because twelve times in succession the story escaped just before it was captured. That's a lot of almosts.

Torn-up grass is not bad, but it is not good. I knew that grubs had gotten into many lawns, mostly from birds dropping the grubs' larvae after they ate them somewhere else. The grubs grow and make a feast of the grass from below. Then more birds, crows and starlings mostly, come and attack the grubs from above. The grass does not stand much of a chance.

But what looks amazing, or terrible, or like voodoo, is that one lawn can be totally destroyed while the grass next door is untouched. That would be called the luck of the larva, unless you have a lawn that did not get lucky. Tony and I saw pie plates and ribbons tied over lawns, and a few front yards that were entirely covered with plastic tarps. That would keep the birds away, but it just let the grubs eat in peace.

However it was the middle of the day and the day was in the middle of the week so there were few people home to ask about their ugly lawns. And the few who were home were angry at their neighbours who were spared. "Not fair," they said. This was not uplifting.

Then Rule Number One came into play.

"Stop," I say to Tony.

"You see a story?"

"No, I see someone with a problem."

"Where?"

"Two blocks back."

It is amazing how slow we can be to recognize something. I thought I saw something, but I wasn't sure. Then, if it wasn't so, why bother even thinking about it? But it might have been. Halfway down a street I thought I saw a blind woman stuck behind a traffic barrier.

I tell Tony I think I saw a blind woman stuck somewhere. That's all it took. He is compassionate. He made a U-turn, on Main Street. It is amazing how fast some of us can be. He speeded up in the new direction and I looked and, yes, there she was, far down a street that was being ripped up for new pipes or repaving or whatever, but it was filled with wooden traffic horses all over the place to keep people and cars safe.

That is, safe if you could see the wooden horses. She was standing behind one with her hand on it trying to move sideways but obviously she could have no idea where she was going. There was no one else on the street.

I started walking rapidly toward her.

"You want me to tape this?" Tony asked.

"No way," I said. The story was not going to be about taking credit for doing what anyone would do. I got to her and she said she was lost. She could not see the construction, she could only feel the dirt beneath her feet and there should not be dirt on the street. She could not even tell where the sidewalk was.

She told me she had recently moved and was trying to get to 39th and Main. I told her about the construction and walked with her to Main Street and pointed out the right direction. How do you point out to a blind woman? I told her it was six blocks in the direction I steered her in. She said she would be fine.

Tony and I resumed our search. We drove south on Main Street for ten minutes, then turned and went north again. Often if you go around the same block three or four times you find something that wasn't there on the first trip.

We drove by 37th Avenue. More construction. And then, the same women, once again trying to go around another barrier, but this one was attached to another barrier and that to another. She was way off Main Street, standing again in the dug-up mud and dirt residue of a side street getting new pipes.

Tony stopped without asking, of course. I got out. He said he could not stay there and would circle the block. I got to the woman. She recognized my voice and this time I walked with her to her destination. That was all. Tony pulled around the corner.

"I found it."

"Found what?"

"The story, you idiot. A chewed-up yard next door to an untouched yard with a man doing gardening in the untouched yard."

"How did you find him?"

"Driving around the block to pick up you."

Nice, when you think about it.

But nothing compared to what happened after "Hello."

"My lawn is okay because I feed the crows. But don't tell my wife," said the man with untouched grass. He was large, white haired, white whiskered and smiling. The last ingredient makes everything look perfect. His name, Bob Balkus.

"I write songs for my wife," he said.

"You what?"

He didn't answer. Instead, he sang:

"You are such a beautiful woman, I would love to marry you. You are sweet as honey."

When he sang, it did not matter that there was no rhyme or orchestra.

"Isobella, I am your fella. You are my surprise in paradise."

He made surprise and paradise sound like the same word.

He said he and Isobella had been married for sixteen years. She was now eighty-seven. He was ninety. Each of their spouses had died of cancer and after that they met.

"I love her more than life," he said. "I write songs to her every day."

He had exercised with a dumbbell so that he could carry his bride across the threshold. And then he sang to her.

It was silly to ask him about his grass.

As Tony and I were leaving, his neighbours got out of a car. Bob is Polish. His neighbours are Chinese. That is what makes the street beautiful, more than flowers.

"So how come your lawn is chewed up and his isn't?" I asked.

"We have no idea. We gave up on ours," they said. "He hasn't done anything. But he is a nice neighbour. It must be magic."

Yes. Or feeding the crows. Or standing out front singing. Or karma. Or luck. Doesn't matter. We had a story of a man who writes songs for his wife, who sadly was not home at that time. We had a story of love, all because of a blind woman. No blind woman stuck behind a barrier, no story.

"I can't put that in this book," I said to Tony after we did another story on the passing of Bert Thomas. (Keep reading. He's the next story.)

"Why not?" asked Tony.

"Because it will sound like I am trying to get credit for helping a blind woman."

"You just did what anyone would do," he said. "You think you should get credit for that?"

Thank you.

47

Bert Thomas

It was just another funeral. Except I was in the rear of the Masons' headquarters on Granville Street. There were four hundred people in front of me. Bert was a popular guy. It was not just another funeral.

The neatest thing was that while a young minister was saying the Lord's Prayer at the front of the crowd, the crowd at the back was buying beer.

"Bert was wonderful." "Bert was everything you want to be." "Bert, I love you."

Those were comments by people at the rear. Obviously, the eulogy at the back was a good match for what was being said at the front.

Just after the Second World War, Bert started hauling lumber out of mills, piling it on a used car and selling it to anyone who would buy it. He worked every day. No sick days, no injury days, no nothing that would stop him from working.

In time he started a small lumber yard on the Fraser River near the Knight Street bridge. It grew into Northern Building Supply, the largest lumberyard in Vancouver. If you walk through it now you will pass many tiny shops where those who are hoping to make a living building windows and doors and window boxes and house framings are working, like Bert did.

It is illegal to live in any of the shops, so no one lives in any of those shops. Bert would only say, "When you make enough you can get a real place to live."

Bert loved everyone. Everyone. He tolerated those who were behind in their rent. He forgave those who could not pay for material. And he ate grilled cheese and fries every day for lunch, until he was in his mid-90s. He ate at TJ's diner, which was balanced above the office in which he worked every day. He worked until he was ninety-five.

When he was younger, back when he was ninety, he did a hundred push-ups, in front of us, in front of the camera. He rode his bicycle around the lumberyard when he was ninety. Then he fell and broke his hip.

After that he was hunched over, but he still climbed the long stairway to TJ's and had his grilled cheese and fries. I brought a friend of mine to lunch to meet Bert. Frank Aicken, who was ninety-four and had started his own lumberyard after the war. Bert was six months older than Frank and the two of them laughed over a burger and grilled cheese and fries and talked of the old days when accounts were kept by pencil on the back of brown paper lunch bags and lumber was delivered by truck or car or shoulder, but it was delivered.

The sight of the two of them walking away from a group of us who were not born when they were working is now part of my DNA. Two old men, Bert with a cane to hold him up, Frank with a white cane because he was basically blind, walking arm in arm, swaying with the pain of age, talking with the joy of youth, until they were stopped by a woman who said, "Bert, do you know I love you?"

A woman, in a lumberyard. When Bert and Frank began, women were at home cooking and changing diapers. Now they were in the yard, picking out seasoned wood. And one of them was in love with Bert.

A few years later came Bert's funeral. His children talked of how wonderful he was, how happy he was, how he taught them to work hard.

In the back of the hall more beer was ordered. The minister was still in the front. The prayers were in the front. Bert was in the back, holding court with the beer drinkers. Even in death, good people make the best stories.

48

The End of the Unfinished Story

It was a long time ago, and it was yesterday. It was the end of the road, but it was the beginning. It was impossible. No, nothing is.

That is relativity, the unfathomable human condition that makes us look at a clock when we are having fun and say "My god, was that really an hour?" It also makes an hour take a year to pass when we have pain, or a year to take forever.

We create our own heaven and hell, hell taking noticeably longer to survive on the relativity scale.

In 2002, which was a long time ago, I wrote in *Back Alley Reporter* about my niece. She was a twenty-three-year-old super turbo-charged model, lacrosse coach, lifeguard and dancer with a ponytail.

Her name is Ashley Lauren Fisher, but she often dropped the last name because Lauren sounded more exciting.

Then one summer day at the beach this outgoing girl with a great future dived off a fellow's shoulders just at the unpredictable instant when the outflow of an extra strong wave reduced the depth of the water from five feet to two and her head hit the hard sand and her neck twisted in the swirling tide and she heard a bang.

Some of you reading this have heard that bang. It was the last time you could feel your face with your own hands. It was the last time you would be able to comb your hair or scratch an itch on your nose or feed yourself or get dressed or go to the toilet or think you could go on living.

But before those impossible-to-climb stone walls became her life, Ashley was still in the ocean. Her body was lifeless, paralyzed, dead. She could not move her arms, her hands, her legs, nothing. Her neck was broken. Water rushed over her face and poured into her mouth and lungs. The undertow of foam and surf rolled her back and forth, pulling and wrenching and tearing whatever might have remained of the spinal cord at the back of her neck. It happened in a moment. Her friend pulled her out while more waves pounded on them.

The next chapter of the story was a massive operation in which doctors replaced the shattered bones in her neck with steel rods. But her spinal cord was crushed beyond repair and beyond hope. She could not breathe. A machine pumped air through a tube that went through a hole cut in her throat.

Because of that machine, she could not talk. She could only mouth words. Not even the air of a whisper was there, only lips trying to form silent words, and when you are standing over a bed with someone you love lying on it, and she is filled with tubes and wires, and you cannot understand what she is saying and she cannot make herself be understood, it is painful for both of you.

"What did you say?"

Looking around the room, "What did she say?"

Looking down, "What did you say? Did you say 'It hurts'? I know it hurts."

More words: "Scared? Yes. We are scared too."

And more: "We don't know. The doctors can't say. But…but… you've got to believe."

And then her eyes closed and her mother and father and brother's eyes wept. She was in intensive care for twenty-nine days, her mind absolutely clear, her body just lying there. Her friends and family stood around her, massaging her arms and legs, trying to keep the muscles alive, but she could not feel us doing it. We tried to be positive, because that is the only medicine we had, but there were many shaking heads, when they were out of the sight of Ashley, and clenched fists and silent prayers said with wet eyes clamped shut.

But each day when the doctors checked her, she would wink at them and smile. She never once whispered, "Why me?" I do not know where she got the courage. It broke my heart in admiration. Because of one wave in the ocean she cannot brush her teeth or comb her hair or walk. She once said to me, "If only I could use my arms."

Rick Hanson can use his arms, and he did the impossible. He went around the world with them and woke up millions to the needs and possibilities of everyone in conditions that once were written off.

There is that relativity again. If only Ashley could use her arms and hands. But nothing below her neck would move. No scratching the nose. No lifting a glass of wine. No chance to live outside of being fed and cared for.

But she was positive. She tried to be positive. She said she would not let this beat her, but so many have said that and ended up losing. She worked on it. But there is just so much positive thought you can take before you realize that no matter what you do, you can never do anything. So she tried to kill herself.

But how do you commit suicide when you can't take pills or

cut your wrists or jump out of a window? Everything has been taken from you, even the ability to get rid of the little breath of life that is still in you. You think your life is unfair? When you can't live, and you can't die, that is unfair.

By struggling and banging in the bathroom she got the shower going. Then she jolted the tub enough to close the plug. Then she waited for the tub to fill. She backed up her power-driven wheelchair, which she operated with a tube to her mouth. She was now off the breathing machine. She would use her breath to kill herself.

She backed it up as far as she could across the room, then blew with all her might into the tube to drive her wheelchair into the side of the tub. Bang, she tilted forward, but not enough. She backed up again and drove harder. Bang. Not enough.

This time she would start at a different angle and get more speed and it would work. The room was filled with steam. The water was dangerously hot. It would be a burning, painful, screaming ending. But it did not matter. She would suck in the scalding water and in two or three minutes she would finish what the cold ocean had started.

She blew and moved, and someone opened the door. "You cannot just go slamming wheelchairs around in a bathroom! Didn't your mother teach you anything?"

Now here the relativity part comes in again, and here's where the positive thinking and positive living comes in. Relative because let's jump ahead ten years. How did that happen so quickly? When you are not living with something and someone they slip slowly out of your mind.

I got an email from Ashley, the outcome of the positive living part that came like the morning after a terrible storm at night.

"There is a publisher who wants me to write a book, but I am not sure what to put in it."

Ashley largely removed herself from her family and started on her own, with no movement below her neck. She pulled and strained and concentrated and the smallest fibre of a nerve that had survived woke up and now she can swing her right arm toward herself. She cannot move it away.

But with that right arm, with a hand that still does not work, she drives her wheel chair.

With her mind and her smile and her personality she manages and is now an owner of a four-star restaurant in Morristown, New Jersey.

She does the hiring and firing. She orders the menu. She circulates around chatting to customers. Business is bursting.

She works with the Christopher Reeve Foundation, giving speeches.

"Living is possible, even when it is impossible."

She helped found a non-profit fashion group, Discovery Through Design, to raise funds for disabled women.

She is a member of the Bonnie Brae Society, one of the country's leading therapeutic learning centres for abused and abandoned youth.

ABC News did a story about her. The *New York Times* did a story about her.

She has a boyfriend. She is again using her family name.

"How did you do all this?" I asked.

She wrote back:

"Do you want the long or short answer?"

Short.

"Honestly, I don't believe in quitting. Disability or not, that's always been me."

I asked her to elaborate, just a bit, because she may have the secret of life.

She added two sentences.

"I think we are all truly disabled in some way, but it's just easier to see some disabilities more than others. Unfortunately my handicap doesn't help my golf game."

I waited ten years to hear that. It was worth it.

Her book? I suggested, "Golf is no longer my game."

49

Under the Zip Line, Another Tale From a Wheelchair

It was a story much like Ashley's, except I was spared the agony of a decade. It was the kind of story you could find every day and go away feeling good.

During the Paralympics a man in a wheelchair was sitting under the Zip Line at Robson Square. His twelve-year-old daughter was with him. You could tell it was his daughter because she stayed close, then ran away, then came back and ran away again.

I know nothing about girls and women, except that's what they do. Boys go away and call a year later. Sometimes they are broke. Girls are more loyal.

"He says he'll be there in five minutes," she said to her father.

He was looking up.

"I hate to bother you, but are you going to ride on that?" I asked.

"I'd love to," he said, "but I'd need someone to carry me and that's not going to happen today."

He told me his name was Stephen and he was waiting for his fourteen-year-old son and his son's friend. He had promised them they could go on the Zip Line before he took them to a sledge hockey game at UBC. It was Canada versus Japan, a sure win for Canada.

Stephen said he had been a dedicated athlete before he broke his neck in a skiing accident when he was nineteen.

"Hard," I said. What else do you say? "Sorry?" He has heard that before. "Awful?" He's heard that too.

"Yes, it was hard. It took a long time to adapt. And you either do that or you don't, and if you don't you do nothing."

He was doing things. He has his own medical equipment distribution company, which he runs from home, and he has two kids and he was going to the big game, which started in half an hour.

"We've been waiting three hours for him to get his twenty-second ride," said Stephen.

"I bet you want to leave," I said.

"I can't do that to him," he said.

"But if he doesn't go soon you'll be late for the game."

Stephen looked up at the line. His cellphone rang. He listened.

"Well, don't worry and have fun," he said. "We'll be watching."

He closed his phone. "They told him it will be another twenty minutes, at least."

"That must hurt, too," I said.

Stephen nodded, but said, "I can't tell him to come down. That wouldn't be fair."

He knew and I knew that they would miss the first period. He had never seen a live sledge hockey game before. I knew by the time they got their car and drove to UBC they could only make it midway through the second period.

"He really wants to do this," said Stephen, looking up at the take-off point where he still could not see his son.

His phone rang again. He listened. "That's tough," he said. "We'll wait."

"They said there would be another five-minute delay."

This was the real game. This was the test of patience and not complaining. This was where you put everything on the line and you did not make someone else feel guilty and you let them have their dream.

"There he is," shouted Stephen's daughter.

His son and his son's friend jumped, screamed, slid across the line, screamed some more, waved, screamed some more and in less than half a minute, counting the time at the end of the run where they were pulled in and got to a safe standing place, it was all over.

"Let's go," said Stephen to his daughter as he grabbed the wheels of his chair and spun around and headed to the bottom of the stairs where the Zip Liners come down.

Slam. He hit a pothole in the middle of the street and was almost thrown out of his chair. He grabbed the wheel and jerked it backwards. This is another game that he plays every day. This is the game none of us who are not there has any idea about. His front wheels were stuck. His daughter came running back, but another man grabbed the back of the chair and pulled him out.

Stephen turned to nod thanks, but the other man seemed to be not even looking for acknowledgement. He was moving off. It was just something he did. That is the kindness that doesn't make someone else feel like they are in need.

The Zip Line veterans came down the stairs. "That was great. That was the best!" Then Stephen's son looked at his father and said, "Thanks."

"We gotta go. We got to go!" said Stephen, but it was obvious the "Thanks" was worth the wait.

"Where's your car parked?" I asked.

"No car," said Stephen as he raced away. "We're taking the bus."

Civic minded. Patient. Cool under pressure. A true athlete. It would have been good if they had seen the first or second period. But by bus they could not have gotten there until the last few minutes of the third. Canada lost.

Stephen won.

50

I Don't See Blackness

This was one of the strangest of stories, and the funniest, and the most touching although the touching scenes were just blackness. And actually, they were not even that.

We took Jessica Rathwell out with us to do a story. She was an intern at the station, in her third year of studying journalism.

Bright, pretty, young, eager, she has all the usual qualities of those who want to be reporters. Pretty is not a requirement, but she has it.

One other thing—she is blind. Totally, absolutely blind. She is not partially blind, not sight impaired, she is blind.

We coaxed her into the story. The veteran cameraman John McCarron, who has had more than his share of hardships in life, bought her coffee and told her this is the way all stories begin, with a break.

We sat on a bench in Confederation Park in North Burnaby. I told Jessica that we often try to do a story about what is right in front of us.

"What about the bocce players?" she asked.

I looked at her. She was staring blindly at her coffee cup.

"How did you know they were there?"

"Well, it's obvious," she said. "Can't you see them?"

"But how did you know they are playing bocce?"

"Are you blind?" she said to me.

"There's a bunch of Italian men and they are yelling and having fun and then it is quiet for a few seconds and then they start arguing again. That's bocce."

She saw more than me.

"Yes, do a story on that," I said.

She walked to them with her guide dog and interviewed them, and the old men playing were patient and funny.

We finished the story with another coffee break. You have to teach her the ways while she is young.

When we put the story on television we never mentioned that she is blind. That had become a side issue. The laugher over the coffee and the characters of the players were more important.

Editor Effie Klein put the story together and described each of the pictures to Jessie. Effie is very good. You really do not need eyes when she tells you what is in the picture.

"Would you like the wide shot that shows all the men or a close-up of the ball to start with?" Effie asked.

"Whatever you think is best," said Jessie.

There is a woman who will go far. When someone else is good at their job you let them do their job, their way. But I suggested that Jessie perhaps say that she sees only blackness but got good vibrations, a good feeling, from the players. That is what she had told me while we were doing the story.

"I can't say that," she said.

I thought she meant she could not say she got a good feeling.

"Why?" I asked.

"Because I don't see blackness."

"What do you see?" I asked, and immediately I knew what a stupid question that was.

"I see nothing," Jessie said.

That is hard to conceive. I close my eyes and see blackness, and I assumed that is what blindness was. Wrong.

Jessie sees nothing. Not even blackness.

And yet, she did the story on the bocce players, and many who watched it did not know she saw nothing of what she was reporting on. She listened and felt. Most who saw the story did not know she was blind.

That is amazing. That is more powerful than those other qualities often sought in young reporters, like the ability to hold a microphone so that the station's call letters can be seen.

But someone in the TV station said it was foolish to say Jessie could be a television reporter. Wrong! That is such a blind way of looking at the job. Remember Rule One.

After I heard that negative comment I took Jessie down to Main and Hastings.

"I've never been here," she said. "It feels scary, and exciting."

But she wanted to get started. Already Rule One was working. The only thing she was worried about was someone trying to pet her Seeing Eye dog. That is forbidden because the dog belongs to her, and only her; kindness, love, affection, loyalty pass between only the two of them, that is how it works. But everyone down here wanted to pet her dog.

No, you can't.

"Why, is her dog too good for us?"

"No, it's a Seeing Eye dog." This is a shock. Seeing Eye dogs don't come down here. "She is blind." That is a shock. Blind people don't survive here.

"Now go and tell your friends not to pet the dog, but you can talk to her."

That is a shock. The gaunt drug addicts looked at Jessie as if she was an alien. And then suddenly, they wanted to protect her. From whom? From each other.

"Hey, she's blind. Be careful, don't crowd her."

She was surrounded by some of the toughest, most lost men and women in the city, the ones whom many people try to avoid. Cameraman John Chant was taping her from a distance, but she did not know that. I said nothing. She probably knew I was still there but she could not be sure.

"Why are you here?" she asked them.

"Because there's nowhere else to go. They don't want us to go away from here."

"Who doesn't?" Jessie was standing up to them.

"The government, the people in charge, everyone is against us," someone said.

Jessie, who only came up to their shoulders, unable to see who she was talking to in a place she had never been, said, "You are just making excuses. Why don't you get a job and do something with yourself?"

She could only hear, "What kind of job could I get? I can't get nothing."

"You're afraid to get a job," she said. She was going for the jugular. "You could do it if you wanted to, so all I see is someone who doesn't want to."

They said very little. I was so proud. After that we took a walk down a back alley past the women and men injecting heroin.

"Are there needles on the ground?" she asked. I had not thought of that.

"There might be."

"Then I won't go any further. I am not risking my dog just to be close to people who have no respect for themselves."

After we left the area she said, "That is so sad. They could all do something but they are there because they are doing nothing."

Jessie left the station and went back to university. Jessie as a reporter? I don't know. She is way too insightful for that job. Maybe she will end up as a leader of a community, a union, a group, a city, because she can see more clearly where she is going than many who can see. Maybe she will look around at a difficult task and say, "Let's throw some light on this situation and solve it."

51

Mona of Trout Lake

She is a jewel. She is a diamond. Finding her made the day sparkle and leaving her made me sad, but I carried away some of her diamond dust and I will keep it and it makes my life richer.

You could find her, just as I did. I was walking around Trout Lake, which I often do because it is a beautiful park literally in the middle of the city. Trout Lake is not the official name of the park. It is John Hendry Park, named after a man who made a fortune owning part of the Hastings Sawmill, which was the sperm cell that entered the forest and started Vancouver. He also owned Trout Lake and, wishing to take advantage of all of nature's bounty, he piped the water from the lake to the boilers at the mill. Later his family gave the lake to the city so long as it was called John Hendry Park. But no one does that. Even the people who live across the street from John Hendry Park call it Trout Lake, which gives you an idea of how unimportant you can easily become. At one end of the lake dogs are allowed to swim and at the other end kids swim. In the middle it has a pump that shoots the water up in the air and probably keeps it healthy enough so the dogs won't catch whatever germs the kids are carrying.

At a picnic bench I said hello to a woman who was having her lunch. That was all it took, one hello.

"Hello," she said.

"Great day," I said.

"Every day here is great," she replied.

"Do you come here every day?"

And here is where one "hello" became a bookmark in life.

"Yes, as a matter of fact, I do come here every day."

I walked closer. "You're kidding."

"No. I've come here every day, for the last twenty years."

"May I join you?" I asked.

Anyone who does anything that long has more than a reason for doing it. They have something deeper, some secret or some love, because you don't stay loyal to anything, not a person or a picnic bench, unless you feel something, unless there is a deep meaning.

"What do you do?" I was waiting for a large answer. I was waiting for "I get in touch with God," or "I commune with Nature," or "I solve the problems of the world."

"I eat my lunch," she said.

I love this woman. I met her five minutes ago and she eats her lunch here almost every day—for two decades. She has grey hair and some wrinkles, but most of all she has a smile.

Her insulated lunch bag was open. I saw she had a screwdriver in it.

"Why do you have a screwdriver?"

"In case someone has a something that needs tightening."

"And the WD-40?"

"In case something is stuck."

This is the person you want to be near if you have a problem.

"I used to go swimming in there when I was a kid, but my mother always said I shouldn't."

"Why?"

"She was worried about us. That's what mothers do. There were no lifeguards then. But she always knew and scolded me because I came home with mud and weeds in my hair."

That was eighty years ago and it was now. Sometimes there is no difference between now and the past. Memories are as real as the place you are currently in. She was still trying to wipe the mud off her head as she spoke to her mother even though I saw none of that. That's one of the magical things of life.

It was a hot day, but not where she sat under a tree. "There's always a breeze here."

I noticed there were no dandelions around her table. It was easy to see because the park is littered with that uncontrollable pesky flower that most of us think is ugly and looks like ragged paper when it goes to seed, but there was none around Mona's table. Why?

"I pull them out," she said, and bent over to remove one that I had not noticed. "You do that enough and you win, without chemicals." Persistence beats poison.

Someone came by on a bike and stopped and said hello. She admonished him for not wearing a helmet. She said later she loved talking to anyone. They joked and he left.

"I was born five blocks from here," she said. "And when I was married we lived three blocks away. I was married for fifty years."

I heard the words but I could not see the memories. "My husband died just two years ago. Sometimes I have my sad days, but mostly I feel good here."

She was eighty-five, she said, but that was hard to believe. A cool breeze and a quiet lunch and a lake to look at don't create stress.

Then she said she had to go to work.

"Work? But you just said you're eighty-five."

She looked at me with pity for someone who did not understand that numbers are one of the least real things when it comes to age.

"Of course I work. You think I could just sit around all day and talk about the old days?"

She volunteered at the food bank in New Westminster where she did just a bit more than simply helping out. She ran the food bank.

"You mean you come here from New West every day to have lunch?"

That's a forty-minute trip, each way.

"Yes. It doesn't seem far," she said.

That's the reason for coming here—the secret, the meaning, the dedication, the love. That's what can't be explained. Those are the bookmarks in life that we keep going back to, so we can relive them.

You can still find Mona there when the weather is good. Go, visit, share your lunch. You will have a good day, guaranteed.

52

Back to Basics

Just to say it again, I get total joy out of finding a story every day. I know I get paid for it, but that will end soon when I retire, and then I will go out and find a story, every day. The joy will be no different. Every day I will meet someone who will say something nice, something fascinating, that even if I had no one to tell it to would make me feel good.

I walked into the sausage shop on Commercial Drive and First Avenue. The name of the shop is strange—no, it is outrageous. I have never seen a name so hard to remember as this: The JN&Z Deli.

"Why do you have such a weird name? And by the way, my nose tells me you have the best bacon and sausages I have ever smelled."

A woman behind the counter said those are our initials. J, the family name, Jeremic, and Natasha and Zoky. "Our father bought this shop and gave it to us."

Oh, my gosh. Once again. I went in to buy bacon and found fascination. You could too.

"This is our shop," said Natasha. "Our father is in the back making coffee, but if you want to do business, you do it with us."

The family had come from Serbia and the father had nothing to give to his daughters. This was the problem in Serbia. It's a problem in many countries. Many people have problems being invaded by others, hated by others and destroyed by others. Serbia was near the top of the list for being knocked to the bottom.

Their father scraped together enough to put a down payment on the shop and taught his daughters to smoke meat.

The same big, old, twenty-foot-high smoker that had been in the back room when he bought it is working seven days a week. Old smokers grow better with age. Zoky, who is the youngest, said, "Look, I used to hide on top of it." She climbed a ladder and got onto the roof of the warm box and looked down.

"It was the best place to sleep."

That is all there is to it, I bought my bacon and it would taste wonderful, I knew that. I had bought it there before, but had never asked about the odd name of the shop.

"Could I meet your father?"

Of course. In the back, just as they said, a Serbian named Savo was making coffee. He had a moustache (what Serbian does not?) and he was brewing the strongest, blackest, coffee I had ever seen (again, what Serbian does not?). He boiled water in a pot on a camp stove, then poured ground coffee into the pot. It boiled. Everything I have ever heard about making coffee from all the fancy coffee-making shops says never boil your coffee.

Savo looked at what he was creating, pondering a moment like a barrister over the boiling pot, and then he picked up his bag of specially ground beans and threw in an extra handful. Perfection. You feel it in your fingers.

"Would you like a cup?" he asked.

I did not know how I could swallow a sip, much less an actual full cup. He did not have demitasses waiting. He had mugs.

And then he took out a bottle of sambuca. Yes, that would add some flavour, but I was working.

Dave McKay, the cameraman I have told you about so many

223

times before, who is a barbecue champ and a country and western singer with his own band and who has long hair, said, "Yes."

Of course he did. That's what makes him a full, living, outgoing, wonderful real person. He and Savo had coffee and sambuca and I had envy. Plus Dave had started at seven a.m. and was off when we finished. After lunch to anyone else was late afternoon to him.

I left that shop with some bacon and a story—two sisters running a smoked meat store. But there was something more here. There was a thrill at learning about them and meeting a guy in the back room with coffee and sambuca. There would be a memory of smells and surprise and laughter.

That was the whole story. Earth shaking? No. Stop the presses? No. The kind of discovery you can tell at dinner about a shop that has the richest, most mouth-watering aroma and is run by two women while their father with a giant moustache is in the back with coffee and sambuca? You bet.

A story sometimes is as tasty as a smoked tenderloin.

I was working with another cameraman a few months later when we stopped to do a story on a pizza shop across the street from JN&Z.

"Go in there a second and just smell," I said.

"Why? We are doing a pizza story, not sausages."

"Just open the door and smell."

"Why?"

"Just smell."

He did. The door closed behind him. I waited. And waited. Finally he came out carrying a heavy bag.

"Let's get the pizza done quick. I want to start eating," he said.

53

Squire's Nutty Horse

"**H**e's retarded," said Squire Barnes, who knows everything there is to know about horses, and if he says a horse is retarded I believe it is certifiably, mentally wacko.

"You can't say that," said Mark Cameron, who was the president of the news union. He stands up for underdogs, even if they are horses.

"Why not?" I asked.

Numerous times I have bet on horses that did not have the sense to know that running requires putting one foot in front of the other. I have called them things that were not complimentary.

"Why? Because we cannot call anyone retarded," said Mark.

In addition to having been the union president, Mark is a video editor who I believe thinks many reporters are somewhat in the same category as Squire's horse, even if he will not call them that.

"But he *is* retarded," said Squire. Squire talks about horse racing as if it is a religion, which it is because if you don't have faith, you are never going to have that heavenly hope of winning.

He is part of a group of believers who pooled their money

to own a racehorse and then discovered that the horse is a non-believer.

"He runs halfway around the track," said Squire, "then stops."

This, I know, is not a good trait for a horse to have after you have paid a great deal of money for said horse.

"He's nuts," said Squire.

"You can't say that," said Mark. "It infers that he is retarded and if we cannot say that about people we cannot say it about horses."

"But the jockey said he just stops," said Squire.

Horses are not supposed to stop when jockeys are on them. Jockeys find that annoying because a horse that stops has trouble crossing the finish line.

"He's crazy," said Squire.

"You can't say that," said Mark. Mark did the negotiating for the union's contract and is stubborn when it comes to interpreting words.

"Crazy is like nuts and nuts is like retarded and we do not use those terms in news anymore."

Squire described the last two races. The horse starts out like a horse. "Then he acts like a human teenager who forgets what he is doing halfway into doing it," he said.

Mark did not come to the defence of teenagers. That takes someone stronger than a union president.

I suggested other words that might describe this heretic who still must be fed and trained and groomed and shod even if he refuses to join in the race that is reason for the grooming and training and shoeing.

Slow?

No, politically incorrect. The days of saying that are long over.

Dumb?

No. He gets fed and shod and housed and brushed and he

doesn't have to do anything in return. That is not dumb.

"He is the only horse I have ever known who finishes a race and isn't tired," said Squire.

That is not supposed to happen. Running is *supposed* to make you tired. Can you imagine a runner in the Olympics finishing who isn't tired?

And after a race, horses get walked until they cool off.

"But he's not hot," said Squire.

"What are you going to do with him," asked Mark.

"Give him another chance," said Squire.

That is the religion of the track—faith even when there is nothing to believe in, pouring money into something when the odds say don't, yelling at a horse who can't hear you, and then pulling out your wallet to do it all again.

"But he *is* crazy," Squire said as he returned to the other sporting news of the day.

Right word, I thought. But it is not the horse who is so dumb.

🐎

There followed another season of losing. Not just losing but trying not to admit that the loser is your horse. No pictures of winners with bouquets and smiles on the wall. No fattening of the wallet. No bragging. Squire would never brag, but it would be nice to say, "Hey, how's the weather and by the way, my horse won." It's like saying my kid got top grades in the piano recital. Except you say my horse smoked the others and won in the stretch. Makes you proud.

But not for Squire.

Two years after he invested in the sport of kings, called that because only kings could afford to feed a loser, I was at the track looking for something to put on television.

There was a table full of flowers outside a barn. That might be good, I thought. "May I ask why your flowers are not planted?"

Craig McPherson looked at me over a battered desk in his office. He was worried about how much feed to give his number three horse to make it number one. Trainers at the track are witch doctors. They look at a horse and say, "Double the feed and ride her hard on the close."

Everyone at the track except jockeys says trainers are the most important part of getting a horse to win. But the truth is jockeys are more choosy about which trainer they work for than which horse they ride.

CEOs downtown have carpeted offices with views of everywhere. CEOs at the racetrack have a room smaller than a single cell in a prison. With no view. In fact, no windows. One door. And many problems. But among them is not the question of where to plant flowers.

"Flowers?"

"Yes, the flowers outside the barn."

"My wife bought them."

"Are you going to plant them?" Actually it is none of my business, but there might be something interesting about flowers at the track, or at least planting flowers at the track.

"No, but you're right. Something should be done with them."

He said he would get one of his grooms or jockeys to do the job. We followed.

"Can't," said the first groom. "Not now," said the second. "Are you kidding? Horses come first," said the third. "Haven't a clue how," said the jockey.

In the end, Craig McPherson, who had thirty-two horses to think about, took the hose and watered the plants. Nice.

Then he said, "Tell Squire we'll try to get him a winner this year."

"What happened to his last horse? The one that wouldn't go fast."

Craig smiled. "He's being ridden by a little girl in Maple Ridge who likes to go slow."

For a person, that would be a brilliant career path. For a horse, Squire's nutty horse, it was super genius.

54

Hospital Stories

Reilly taught me you never have to be sick if you don't want to be, and that is true. But positive thoughts only make you feel good, keep the sniffles away and relieve the flu. They don't stop your insides from getting twisted, especially when you don't know it is happening. After a non-malignant tumour pulled some of my small intestines into my large bowel the bowel got upset and twisted around like a knotted garden hose. I knew nothing about this until I woke one morning with, to say the least, an uncomfortable feeling in my stomach. Actually, it was equivalent to dying under the wheels of a train. But I was lucky—I not only lived through it but I got a chance to write some stories about being in a hospital:

YES, YOU CAN SAY THE F WORD

It is the most important thing, they told me.

"If you don't do it we don't know if the operation was successful."

"But I can't, and if I could I couldn't here," I said.

"Then you can't go home."

In Lions Gate Hospital I was told that repeatedly. In fact, it was all the medical volumes squeezed into one juicy, living, self-descriptive, non-Latin word.

"If you pass gas—you know, 'FART'," said the serious-looking nurse, "then we know things are as they should be and you can go."

I was on the ward where many of the customers had had something repaired or removed from somewhere below their hearts and above their crotches, a rather large area in which farting appears to be the approved foolproof method of diagnosing progress.

My path to this insight began on a Saturday morning when I awoke with severe pain in that British Columbia (which is larger than Texas) -sized region of the body.

"You should go to a clinic," said my wife.

"No," I said, even as I felt the chilling cutting and stabbing pain like losing a sword fight. "I'm a guy. It will pass."

Instead, I opted to go with her to the library.

"You look like you are in really bad pain," she said.

She may have gotten that idea because the steering wheel was starting to crack under my twisting fingers.

"Not me," I said.

"Please try a clinic."

"Don't need it."

At that moment we were passing Lions Gate and the thought came to me that if I did go to a clinic I would die before my number was called and then they would send my body to the morgue in the hospital anyway so I might as well stop. Besides, there was a parking spot available.

Three hours later I was in the operating room. The last thing I heard someone say to someone else over my stretcher was, "He MUST have this operation today. It can't wait until tomorrow."

I figured the library was out.

Seven hours later I woke up in a bed with six bottles of stuff dripping into me through tubes and one tube draining stuff out of me. I was not sure where I was, or who I was, or even if I was, but one of the first things I remember hearing was, "Do you feel like passing gas?"

We few special people with adjusted and reduced internal plumbing on that floor were asked that by every nurse and every doctor every hour. There would be many variations on the same theme.

"Farted yet?"

"No."

"Tooted?"

"No."

"Passed gas?"

"Not yet."

"Blew wind?"

"No."

"Made vapour?"

"No, no, no, but I'm trying."

"Heard anything?"

"Not yet."

By the third day my abdomen, which had had so much removed from it and was consuming nothing but liquids, was growing. I could feel it. I could see it. I had a large honeydew melon from a BC hot house inside me.

"Anything?"

"Not yet."

By day four I had a watermelon from a sweltering Mexican field under my skin. A watermelon that if you swallowed without chewing would kill you. It was killing me.

My wife said that did not look good.

"Oh, no," I said. "It's natural."

My wife asked a nurse if someone could make a hole to let the gas out.

"There already is a hole," said the nurse. "Just tell him to use it."

Once again I was going to die. Then my roommate in the next bed wished me good luck and said he would cross his fingers.

His name was Richard Peterson and he was having a catheter installed (see next story) because the one nature gave him had gotten too narrow to do what it was supposed to do, which is highly uncomfortable, especially if someone impatient is standing behind you at the urinal.

He suffered a stroke when he was a fifty-seven-year-old construction worker. He was eighty-one now. He had not let the stroke stop him even though he could use only one arm, and one leg did not function nearly as well as the other.

I went into the bathroom and thought about him going through all that. That was one powerful pair of crossed fingers on the other side of the door.

Toot!! Blaaaaaa!!! Phhhhhhhhblu!!!!! Brrrrrrughhhh!!!!! and again, Toot! just for good measure.

I opened the window, then opened the door. "Richard, you saved my life!"

The news spread. On the sixth floor east wing of LGH there was applause. Honest to heaven, the first toot gets cheers and high fives.

"It's the sound of Christmas lights lighting up," a nurse said, even though we all know Christmas lights don't make sounds and toots don't light.

Clap, clap, clap. I took a bow, because I could, now that the watermelon had vanished as if it was on a picnic with kids on a steamy afternoon.

With all the bad things we are taught about passing gas, "You can't, you shouldn't, not here, not now," I have learned it is the star of the gastro-intestinal tract. If your farts are fine you can bet everything is fine. If they're not, cross your fingers and try to toot.

Sometimes medical problems, like life, can be so simple to understand and deal with if you just let it happen naturally and don't worry about what others will say.

SOMETHING ELSE YOU DON'T WANT TO KNOW

"Lay back, spread your legs and relax."

It was two a.m. and with my hospital gown pulled up I was naked. A pretty nurse stood over me holding a long piece of plastic tubing.

"What are you going to do?"

"Put this in your penis."

"No you're not."

The shudder is still going through me.

"I'm afraid so. You are having trouble going. This will solve that," she said.

Solve nothing, I thought. Do you see how fat that tube is?

"Relax. You're not relaxing," she said.

"I AM RELAXING."

"No you're not. Your legs are breaking the bottom of the bed."

I had heard about this. I had heard that to get urine flowing they do strange things to you in the name of compassion. But I know what's possible and what's not, and putting a plastic tube like they use in fish tanks to pump air into the water into the tiny opening at the end of my penis is impossible. Besides, I had taken biology in high school and nowhere did I ever see a picture of anything going into there.

"How do you do it?" I asked.

"Easy, we just squeeze the tip and slide it in."

Ouch. Please, not today.

"I'm having trouble," said the nurse.

YOU'RE having trouble? What about me?

"If you don't relax it won't go in right."

There was something wrong about what she was saying, or maybe it was just wrong who was saying it.

"Take a deep breath, then let it out."

I inhaled half the air in the room.

"Now let it out."

"NO," I thought. If I do I know what's going to happen.

"Breathe."

No.

Every man friend who has asked me about the operation has only been interested in hearing about the catheter. They listen, and shudder, and then say they don't want to hear about it. Every woman friend has said, "So what's the big deal? It's just a tiny tube."

"Women love this," a nurse told me. "They don't have to get up to go to the bathroom. But men hate it."

Gee, there's a surprise.

I couldn't hold my breath any longer. I was trying, but I couldn't. Poooof. The air came out and I know what happened, even though I was staring at the ceiling.

"Ohhhhhhhhhhhhhhhhh."

That was me, if you didn't guess.

"Ohhhhhhh."

"There, it's all over, you big baby. It didn't hurt, did it?"

Hurt? Well, no, it didn't hurt. But on the other hand I looked down and there was a fish tank tube sticking out of a place where no tube has ever been stuck before. Hurt has nothing to do with it. The impossible has everything to do with it. It's a fish tank tube, sticking out of me. That is more important than hurt.

It was working. I could feel that. What was in me was coming out and going into a plastic bag. You don't want to know about that, either. I asked how much was inside. About nine inches. Ouch, again.

That would sound like bragging, but not, sadly. That was nine inches inside me going to my bladder, reducing the inches on the outside significantly.

And when the catheter was finally removed, the same process, backwards. Legs spread, deep breath, then hand over hand, or finger over finger pulling up the line like fishing. There was another long vowel that came from deep inside me and out my lips.

I had never felt anything like that before, and every other time I had ever said that I'd had a new feeling I had secretly wished to feel it again. This was different.

All of this is told just to let you know that if you are a guy and it happens to you, you will survive. You just won't forget it.

If you are a woman you will just shake your head and think men are such wimps.

EATING IN BED

"I apologize, here's your lunch."

That would be the nice waitress delivering a meal to my bedside.

Next came dinner. "Sorry about this. I wish I could get management to eat it."

The next day I spoke to one of the servers in the hallway: "I put down the food and leave as quickly as I can. I don't want them to see it before I am out of the room."

In a hospital, dining critics are as numerous as unfinished meals.

"What's this?"

"Shepherd's Pie."

"My butt it is. It's a mess."

"Sorry. On the menu it says Shepherd's Pie," said the server.

My cellmate looked at it. He was English. They invented Shepherd's Pie.

236

"This is what gets scraped off the plates after we have Shepherd's Pie," he said.

"Taste it," he said to his wife. "No," she said. "It's scary."

"Would you like some?" he asked me through the thin curtain that gives everyone all the privacy a human with tubes stuck in him would ever need.

"I'd love to," I said, "but I'm on all liquids all the time."

"Pity," he said, "But on the other hand, do you have any Jell-O left over?"

But there is another approach to hospital food. Remember Rule One.

Hospital food is worth dying for on Day One, the morning after the operation:

Menu, FULL FLUID.

One pack of sugar, white.

One cup of water, hot.

One Jell-O, red.

One bag, tea.

Yummy. I could never have come up with this on my own. First, variety. Hot water, cold Jell-O, what a combo. And white sugar, like putting forbidden fruit in front of me. I thought white sugar was bad, that if you ate it you would end up in a hospital. But now, white sugar from the hospital. This is pushing the culinary envelope. Lions Gate food rocks.

I should put the tea bag in the hot water. They are very thoughtful not to do it ahead of time since it might be too strong.

Oh, my, isn't this considerate? They were fooling about the water being hot. They don't want burned fingers in a hospital. The water was nicely almost warm, not quite warm but not cold. The tea would be an experience. This happens in college dorms when a boy having trouble standing, or seeing after a night of swallowing beer and whisky and wine mixed together,

237

accidentally picks up a cup which he thought had watered down whiskey but instead was the tea left behind four hours earlier by a girl who said she would not be part of such debauchery. And then he drinks it.

The effect is instant. It creates wakefulness in an otherwise sleepy young man. Suddenly he is shouting in tongues and dancing. And then he puts the tea back into the glass and on the floor. Room temperature tea is not for the timid, or the intoxicated.

But first, Jell-O. I learned to spell with J-E-L-L-O.

"Hey kid, can you spell yet? In grade one you know you have to be able to spell."

"Of course, sir, I can spell. J-E-L-L-O."

"Can you spell it without the dashes?"

"Yes, sir, but that's cheating."

"Can you spell anything else?"

No. There isn't anything else that needs spelling. You see, once you could spell Jell-O and read Jell-O your parents never asked you to learn another word because Jell-O was the cheapest thing on the shelf.

Back in the hospital, after Jell-O and tea I still had that packet of sugar. I hid it in case lunch was late.

But it wasn't. It never is. No matter what you wish.

Lunch was way different. Green Jell-O, with water, hot, bag, tea, and sugar, white.

"I can't wait. Green Jell-O. Be still my aching taste buds."

Then dinner. Jell-O, red, water, hot, bag, tea, but also nourishment, soup, broth, beef. Except there was something besides heat missing from the soup. It was the beef, and the broth.

"Lucky you," said my cell mate through the curtain. "You have liquid. I have meat loaf. It is not meat."

But at the end of the week I had only praise for my diet. I had lost weight and stayed alive. My guess is neither of those things would have happened if I had stayed home. So, to the chefs of Lions Gate, thank you. And one of the first things I did when I got home was teach my granddaughter how to spell J-E-L-L-O.

And then she asked with pure innocence, "What is Jell-O?"

DID YOU SLEEP WELL?

It is a pleasant, sweet voice at six-thirty a.m.

"And how did you sleep last night?"

You stare at the pretty face. You've heard the nice question. Answer: No one on earth can answer that. This is a hospital.

The ice machine is right across the hall from the room with my cellmates and me. The machine is behind a door with a sign: Please Keep This Door Closed, obviously because the ice machine makes a lot of noise when the chunks fall into plastic cups, which need to be filled all night. But the trick is to open the door with your shoulder so you get no germs, then reach into the machine. You keep your foot against the door to hold it open while you hold your cup under the spout that lets the chunks clunk and clash and clamour. It is hard to describe the sound of falling ice at two a.m.

Add some water and pull your foot away and go back to work and the door closes around the resting, now quiet machine. And see, the door was never really open.

And then the next ice-hungry person comes. And the next. The fuel of the night shift in a hospital is ice water, which is very healthy, unless you are getting it by ear.

At two a.m. my new companion in the next bed, Cully, who is ninety and was in the Battle of the Atlantic, pushes his call button. His bed is wet and he did not do it. His IV has come out and his personal saline solution is dripping on his sheets. It is a rule of life that you cannot sleep with saline-soaked sheets.

The very nice nurse comes but cannot get the IV back in.

Cully's veins were hard to find during the day. At night they are close to impossible. The nurse calls another nurse. I listen from behind the curtain and make good wishes for Cully. Eventually, they get it fixed, and somehow give him a dry sheet, which is good and kind. I close my eyes.

Then there is a Code Blue. The speaker is on the wall, inside our room. Someone is dying and will be saved and that is good. But that someone is not in our room.

Code Yellow. The speaker speaks. Someone needs the key for the narcotics cabinet. I am glad they keep the drugs locked up because right now someone in our room would be taking them to get the sound of the speaker out of his head.

"Julie. Call."

Julie has a phone call. I know, because out of the darkness of the night the speaker that I can almost reach on the wall behind my head has spoken, again. It is an important call because Julie is a nurse and someone needs her and wherever she is she will hear the need and answer it.

"Mitchell, telephone."

Three a.m. Mitchell is a nurse. He has treated me for two nights. He is upbeat and wonderful. But now he has a call and he will be wonderful to someone else's needs. Since I am awake I am hoping the someone else's needs are not too bad.

"Ruth, call." Three thirty a.m. Since I am still awake I now have someone else to wish good things for.

More ice.

Two rooms away someone is dying. Of course they are—that's one of the things hospitals are for. You are born here and die here. I am lucky. They postponed the second part of that for me. Hospitals are good for that. But since this person is on the way out, the time restrictions are not enforced for visitors. And that is as it should be. They are kind and understanding in the hospital.

240

Some of the visitors to the room two rooms away from me are crying and sobbing and wailing and chanting. It is their religion to make outward sounds and this is as it should be, bringing comfort to those staying and the one going.

The chants are very nice. I listen to them. They mingle with the sirens outside. The fire department is across the street. They keep their sirens down, for the sake of the hospital, but they turn them on briefly, for the sake of safety, when they pull out to save someone who will be brought back to the hospital by ambulance, with a siren, which they shut off as far away as possible. Just there down the street I can hear it shut off, again.

"Sorry to wake you. Oh, you are awake. Good. We have to check your vitals."

Pump. Squeeze. "Put this under your tongue."

"You can go back to sleep now."

Ice machine. Siren. Speaker. Ice machine.

And then, six-thirty a.m. and the sweet voice with the question. "How did you sleep?"

Well, you know the answer: "Just fine."

ONE DEGREE OF SEPARATION

I looked at them in the hallways of old folks homes, and long ago in Riverview, and on their front porches and in supermarkets and standing at bus stops, lost.

They were unsmiling, unwashed, unshaved, uncombed. They were confused, wandering aimlessly or sitting aimlessly, not sure where they were or where they were going. They broke my heart. They break yours because you say this is not skid row. These people are not drug addicts or hopeless alcoholics. They did not willingly arrive at this place.

I did stories about them, trying to understand how they went from strong, upright citizens, taxpayers, parents and gardeners to older, accident prone, dishevelled, lost and sad. Of course it does not happen to everyone. Thankfully most of us hang onto ourselves up until the end, giving up as precious little as possible. But it does happen. Just look at the little old lady with her grocery bag standing at the corner as the light changes to walk, then don't walk, then walk and she still hasn't moved.

We are helpless. We who watch them can't remember something we know nothing about: their past, which was when they were themselves.

And then I had this emergency surgery. This is the last story about that. This is the only one that really matters. The details are irrelevant. What is important is afterwards I woke up in extreme pain and had a fish tank of drugs running through my body to bring down the feeling of cutting into my abdomen and stopping my infection. I awoke not knowing which way was up. I only knew one button on one cord lying on my bed—the yellow button for pain. I did not take my finger off it.

On the first day: "Can you try to stand?"

"Stand?"

"Yes, stand. It's good for you. You've got to get moving."

"Stand?"

"Try it."

This is the good not-so-new method to get you moving right after an operation. No more resting in bed until you get better. Get up and chase after the feeling of being better. It is a wonderful method, which I know works.

"Stand?"

My legs would not do it. My head would not do it. I had no idea how to do it. My insides hurt.

"Try getting your leg over the side of the bed."

Along with all the grunts and owwws one toe came down on the floor. "Oh, God." Two toes. "God in heaven."

"Can you stand?"

If this is a reality show, you, dear nurse, are a goner. As soon as I can stand I'm going to kill you. Of course, I didn't think that. I couldn't think anything. I was trying to follow directions and look for the yellow button.

By the third day I was walking the hallway, with both hands on the pole on wheels that carried my five bags of stuff dripping into me and the one bag of stuff dripping out. I had not shaved for three days, or washed, even though the nurses were good and tried to clean me. I had not washed or combed my hair.

I was not taking steps. I was sliding my slippers slowly, but not in any direction I could follow and sometimes one foot got caught behind the other and I had to stop. How do I get that foot out and in front? I was lost.

I stopped by an empty stretcher in the hallway. My hospital gown was falling off my shoulder. There were two pairs of snaps on it and only one was together. With my pole hanging with bags standing next to me, with my body odour rising and hair a mess and unbrushed teeth feeling fuzzy I tried to push two snaps together, and couldn't. I tried again and again. I couldn't.

I was one of the lost people I had done the stories about and three days of pain and drugs was all that had passed. If you have been through this, you know. You disappear. In a few days I would be me again. I was lucky. My operation was a success and I would be fine.

This does not tell me how those people at the bus stops and the grocery stores who cannot pull their coats over their shoulders or have not shaved or who put their lipstick on crooked got there. It could happen so quietly, unexpectedly, quickly or slowly. But it doesn't matter. It happened and they are there, lost.

The only thing it tells me is we are them, or we could be them, and it would have nothing to do with making wrong choices or doing stupid things. The other thing it tells me is to help them get their coats over their shoulders, and ask if they are lost and offer to help.

Someone helped me with the snap. It was the nicest thing in the world.

55

The Hollow Tree

Lt is not good to have a prejudice against anything, because that means not only are you stupid, but you can miss a real good story.

I hate the Hollow Tree in Stanley Park. It is a pale, poor skeleton of its original massive beauty and it should be put to rest.

When it was close to collapsing after one of the big storms I was happy. I thought it should be laid on its side and turned into a giant planter, giving life to others. But no, some do-gooders came along and said they will raise lots of money and stand that dead hunk of shrivelled wood up and brace it with steel beams and make it look all good again.

Phooey. Sometimes do-gooders try to do too much good, and you know too much of a good thing can be bad, at least to someone who has a prejudiced viewpoint, like me.

I have seen pictures of the giant red cedar in its glory when the bark was four feet thick, which made the hole in the middle of the tree seem like a tunnel. I have seen the pictures with kids climbing on the sides of the tree while a carriage filled with people was inside the tree. And there are pictures of famous people like Pauline Johnson, Canada's first poet, swallowed up by the tree. They are all beautiful pictures and there are many of them because the tree was the first tourist attraction in the park.

After the park was dedicated it was really just another place filled with trees, nothing else. But it was a park. Of course, right outside the park there were trees just like inside the park. What really was the point of going to a park? Good question, until the Hollow Tree was discovered and a road was built around the park to get to it. Now we had somewhere to go and something to see.

It was the site of the first popcorn vendor, and the first tourist photographer, hence all the great pictures.

There are thousands of hollow cedar and hemlock trees in British Columbia. It happens when their centres rot away. They make cozy places for bears to hibernate. But when one is big enough to back a carriage into and it is conveniently next to a road in a park it becomes a great tourist attraction. The tree grew tall and strong and had a happy life for almost eight hundred years. Then it became famous. Then like all things, it died. Almost no one alive now has ever seen the tree while it was in a similar condition to themselves, alive. And after it died kids did what kids do. They went inside the hollow part and said this is cool, what can we do with it? So they set fire to it.

Over the last half-century its barky flesh dried up and fell off until it became a skeleton of a tree. And then to add more insult to it, a hemlock sprouted behind it and before anyone noticed the hemlock was looking like a fat telephone pole growing out of the rear end of the famous old stump and was pushing it forward. These were not its glory days.

But more problems were coming. The big wind of 2006 that knocked down ten thousand trees in the park almost pulled the Hollow Tree out of the ground. It was starting to tip and the Park Board said it had to go. You can't have a headline that says: Dead Tree Makes Tourists The Same.

Then came the Do-Gooders.

"Let it die," I said. I didn't say it to them. I said it to myself, but I was sure wishing they heard my thoughts.

"No," they said.

They raised hundreds of thousands of dollars and got it standing upright held by steel poles.

"Okay, have it your way," I said. Yes, it looks much better. But it's still not like it was back in the old days before I saw it. That's how prejudice is born. You follow some thought put into your head from a time before your head was born. But it did not look like the old pictures so my mind was made up. I didn't like it.

I sounded like some Southerners I met in Alabama in the 1960s when we were discussing race relations: "Ain't never gonna be good," they said.

Well, of course they, prejudiced as they were, were wrong.

Me, prejudiced as I was, was right. I did not like the new Hollow Tree. It was not like the old Hollow Tree.

Then a cameraman named Chester Ptasinski and I were cruising around the park one day when we saw not one, not two, but three photographers taking pictures of two people in front of the tree.

"Stop." And all the usual stuff.

"Who, why, etc." All the usual stuff.

They were a television crew from Korea doing a documentary on British Columbia because, "it is such a wonderful place."

I agreed. And also I thought how lucky I am. We will do a story about them doing a story. What more could I ask? They were thinking the same thing. They had a local reporter who could tell them something about anything—it hardly matters what—fall into their laps.

They asked me about the tree. Uh oh. Okay, I'll tell them about how it used to be, how beautiful and majestic it was. I showed them with my arms how thick the bark was. They were impressed. Then I thought a wonderful modern television-age thought.

In the story I would do about them I would include pictures of how the tree used to look and they could take the pictures off the television and use them. They were thrilled. Suddenly they had something they were not searching for and they knew it would look good. The young woman who spoke English asked me if this tree represented anything of the spirit of Canada.

Stuck. I can't suddenly take away what I had given them. I can't tell them I did not like the tree. After all, who cares what I think. They were looking at a magnificent part of the natural and spiritual past of this country.

I said: "This tree is like the soul of Canada. It is strong and even when it is down, it gets up again. And best of all, some wonderful people raised money on their own to make it stand again. They took no tax money. They did it because they wanted to make it better for everyone."

Actually, everything I was saying is what Canada is to me, and you. It is a good, strong place that helps others.

"This could be the symbol of Canada," I said. "It's been through a lot of hardships, but you can't keep it down and it welcomes everyone."

Suddenly I loved this old, gaunt stump and the people who worked to stand it back up. It had taught me a lesson: If you don't like something just because you don't like it, turn around and slap yourself because you are an idiot.

56

Pipeline Road and Can't We Get This Right?

Along time ago there was a lagoon right at the entrance to a park that was still being proposed in which also lived a hollow tree.

No one who wanted the park knew about the tree as yet because there were no roads leading to it. But that beautiful lagoon was a gem.

"Look, it fills with water then half empties its water with the tide," someone in officialdom probably said, because those are people who sometimes can see what is right in front of them.

"Of course it does," said a person who was not an official. "It's a lagoon, you idiot. Lagoons fill with water and empty their water with the tides. That what makes it a lagoon."

"Regardless of the reason, it will be a beautiful part of our new park," said Mr. Official.

Then came the day when they pronounced and dedicated the park and called it Stanley after the man who was the Queen's representative, and it was a beautiful thing. Lord Stanley said the park is open for all people.

And then they started to change it.

"We need a grand entrance," said Mr. Official. "And it should be right here, at the end of Georgia Street," which was just a dirt road.

"But if you put the entrance there it will cut off the lagoon," said the non-official.

"Piff, puff," said Mr. Official.

So they dug up a lot of seashells and discards and dirt from a Native midden (which would later be called a historic site and what was left of it was made off-limits). And they dumped the shells and discards and dirt across the neck of the lagoon to make a road and entrance to Stanley Park.

"Nice road," said Mr. Official.

"But the lagoon cannot fill up and empty out," said you know who.

At the same time the most famous poet in Canada was paddling her canoe around the lagoon. Pauline Johnson was half Native and half white and totally smart and a really cool poet. She performed all over Europe and America and Canada, wearing buckskins and frilly dresses, as a woman who lived in two worlds would do.

She wrote amazingly beautiful poetry about the land and its people and animals and trees. And she wrote about the lagoon, which was no longer a lagoon. She called that poem The Lost Lagoon, because it was lost as a lagoon. She is also the only person officially buried in the park. You can visit her resting place in the trees across the road from the Tea House restaurant on the way down to Third Beach. If it is possible to be happy about where you are buried, she is ecstatic.

For more than a hundred years since, it has been called Lost Lagoon.

250

"Why is it called Lost Lagoon, mommy? It's not lost," a little one says today, walking around it with her mother.

"I have no idea," replies her mother. "Why don't you Google it?"

But back up a hundred-plus years.

"Boy, that stinks," said Mr. Official. "Can't something be done about it?"

"Of course it stinks," said his non-official friend. "It is full of seawater and fish and crabs and they are all dead and stinking because it cannot drain any longer."

"Well, strike a committee and fix it," said Mr. Official, who was holding his nose as he went off to another free official dinner of salmon. "Golly, I wish they would serve a steak for a change. Every visitor wants salmon. I am so tired of it. I wish I lived in Alberta."

So a committee figured that they must get the water in and out of the lagoon that was lost, but not really.

"Let us put in pipes that will flood the lagoon at high tide and empty it at low," a person who was not an engineer said.

As soon as they raised the funds by increasing taxes they started laying large pipes from Burrard Inlet to the lagoon. It was a shorter distance to the beach that would later be named Second Beach (they were not very inventive with names), but sometimes the tide went out too far and the pipe would have to go on forever and that would be ugly.

So they laid a pipe from Burrard Inlet to the lagoon.

It got clogged. The fish and the crabs and the sand and seaweed could not figure out how to get through a long, pitch-black pipe and so they got stuck. And then more got stuck behind them.

The pipe had to be cleaned out frequently and that was not fun. They had to have special pipe-cleaning city employees who complained their work was stinky, if not dangerous.

251

Folks living in the park, of which there were many, used the pipe as a roadway. "Meet you on the pipeline," they would say.

Time passed, and the son of Mr. Official said, "We need to do something about that lagoon. It still stinks and the pipe is always filled with things that are yucky and someone should do something."

So they drained the lagoon that was not a lagoon. Then they put in more pipes on the other side of the lagoon that was now a pond. The new pipes came from the city's sewer system, but not the sewers that carried gunky stuff. This was the runoff from the streets, and it filled up the lagoon with clean rainwater.

Now it was not only not a lagoon that did not drain, it was not a lagoon, because it did not have seawater in it, which a lagoon must have to deserve such a name. The dictionary decides that. But the name stuck. It was and still is Lost Lagoon. And the original solution was covered over and turned into a road called Pipeline Road. And it still has a pipe beneath it. Imagine that.

The only other secret note about Lost Lagoon is that so many people in Vancouver love it they want to spend eternity there. They walk around it in their days of life and when they die they ask their children to spread their ashes around their beloved lagoon.

And the children do that, despite it being illegal. You cannot spread ashes on any public land, that's a no-no. But forget that. We all do it. That is part of Rule Number Two: Continuity is for wimps. That means you should make up your own rules.

However, so many people follow Rule Number Two that the banks of Lost Lagoon are covered with the remains of the beloved dead. That makes it too slippery for park workers to tend the plants along the edge of the lagoon that is not a lagoon. Sometimes they slip and fall in. That is very dangerous since the water is so polluted that a report has to go immediately to WorkSafe BC. There is nothing simple in life.

So a special, secret crew is dispatched early on occasional mornings to shovel up the beloved remains and take them to the recycle dump, which is a perfect place. It almost makes you into a Buddhist.

Meanwhile, Lost Lagoon continues to be one of the most beautiful places in the park. Forget that it is not a lagoon, and that it is not lost. If you walk around it you still feel like writing poetry.

57

The Dead President

This is the coolest scandal in the history of the park, even though it had nothing to do with the park. It's about death and maybe murder and intrigue and a cover-up. That makes it page-one news. I covered stuff like this when I was a police reporter.

"Listen, chief, the President of the US was poisoned and it happened right here in Vancouver and I have some of the facts, although I can't prove anything."

Warren Harding was President of the United States from 1921 to 1923. You notice that is not four years. And he was not shot.

But pushing aside all niceties, he is widely regarded as having been the worst president in the history of the US. It had something to do with corruption and graft, which are not the best of qualities. In his personal life he was said to be a philanderer, a frequent philanderer. His wife was said to be not happy about this.

He was also said to have been inducted into the Ku Klux Klan in a secret ceremony in the White House. Others say that was probably not true, which is a profound relief.

But one thing positive he did: he visited Canada, and he was the first US president to do so. Of course it was just a fluke. He wanted to visit Alaska and on the way back his ship put in at Vancouver. President Harding wanted to wow the quaint foreign folks, and have a plate of salmon.

Before lunch he spoke in Stanley Park, at Brockton Oval. Because he was the American president, 50,000 people showed up to listen. He said we were good neighbours. Then he went to lunch in the Hotel Vancouver.

Salmon, of course.

Afterwards he played golf with very important people. He wore knickers. They all wore knickers. But by the sixth hole he was feeling terrible. He had a pain in his stomach. He was doubling over.

He did not want to appear weak, so from the sixth hole they moved to the seventeenth, and then played the final shots. He wanted the newspapers to say he finished the game.

He and his entourage left that night for Seattle. By the time they got there the White House homeopath was looking into his pained face. They were going to stop in Portland but decided to keep their train going to San Francisco where there would be better medical help.

It didn't help. He was dead by the time the train stopped.

There are many theories as to what happened. It may have been some of his enemies, of which he had many, who poisoned the fish he had for lunch. That would be easy to do since they were in a foreign country and there was less security, actually none in the kitchen.

Or his wife might have said you have philandered once too often and she might have slipped into the kitchen.

It would have been easy to tell what killed him if they had carried out an autopsy. However, his wife forbade that and had his remains embalmed six hours after he died.

The official records say it was heart problems. Could have

been. Sounds better than underhanded slipping of something onto his salmon. We will never know.

What we do have is his head in a bronze relief on a slab of marble right behind where the audience sits to watch Theatre Under The Stars.

More than sixty years later Bill Clinton went for a jog in the park. There is no statue of him. He brought his own cook.

58

Motorcycle Childhood

Every Tuesday I have coffee with Harold. I have written about him in two books.

I met Harold after he sent me a handwritten letter asking if he could record some stories from my books for a friend of his who was blind.

Of course, I said. I was honoured.

We met one day. He drove his motorcycle to the meeting. He was eighty-nine then.

His history, in short, is he wanted to be a dentist after the war but had no money. During the war he had flown in Mosquito night fighters over the English Channel as a radar technician. Afterwards, counting all his pay and war bonds, he didn't have enough money to fill a pocket much less pay tuition at dental school.

So he and his brother decided to build a house in Vancouver to raise the money, even though they had no idea how to build houses.

I apologize if you have read this before, but a good story never grows old. The amazing thing is Harold and his brother went to a friend who had just gotten out of the army and who knew how to build houses. This friend, Frank Aicken, told them over coffee and sandwiches how to clear the land and lay the foundation. The next day they did that, then more coffee and instructions and they framed the house, then after much more coffee and sandwiches and without a formal plan or apprenticeship training or overtime charges they finished it.

It was sold and all the money went to dental school. No licence, no regulations, no greed. Everything went to the education of one.

Then I learned that the man he was making the recordings for was that same fellow who taught him how to build the house. So touching. The house is strong. It is still standing and in use in Vancouver. Frank, his friend who told him how to built it, is blind and listens to the recordings that Harold brings him.

Harold is now ninety-two. He has had to give up his motorcycle because he broke his hip tripping over his walker. His daughter told him no more zoom zoom on his bike. He told her that he tripped over his walker, not his motorcycle and he should give up the walker.

We meet at Tim Hortons in North Vancouver at eight-forty-five a.m. and no matter what time I get there he is always there before me. He buys the coffee, and I sometimes bring him corn muffins I have made an hour before. He tells me stories, about the depression and riding the rails as a hobo and cutting down trees by hand, and lots and lots about the war.

But what I like best is his childhood.

Sitting across the table is an old man, a very old man. He still smiles, he still has the strength to drive a car and live on his own and bring astronomy magazines to show me pictures of the stars, in which he is very interested, but he is an old man.

And then, sometimes, while he is talking he goes back to when he was ten years old and living in Kitsilano.

"The sidewalks were made of wooden planks. They were about twelve feet long and held up on blocks of wood," he said. And then he saw himself and his brother walking on the planks, after a rainfall.

"We would wait until someone was walking toward us and then we'd jump on the boards and make them bounce and they would hit the mud puddles below and splash up." And then he laughed. Of course it was nasty and they were rotten kids, but Harold was living more than eighty years in the past, and it was right now.

"Sometimes we got caught and we would get spanked," he said. "If mother did it, it didn't hurt so much." He smiled. The memory was more than a memory. It was reality across a coffee table. It was something we all have, when we are travellers through time and space.

"And once when I got a dime for church but spent it on candy my father caught me." There was still a smile, but it was different. He remembered his father getting extremely angry and putting the candy back in the bag and taking both it and him back to the candy store. "He got the money back. I don't know how because I had eaten some of it," said Harold. "And he told the man in the store never to sell me any candy again. Then the ten cents went to church."

He was frightened then and he was still frightened now at the memory. He is a very old man who was shot at during the war and rode a motorcycle at ninety and he was still frightened by his father who did not like what he did with his church money. Our past is our present, meaning everything we do or is done to us becomes us.

But the story I liked best was one of the little trips in a tiny dinghy he and his brother and friends would take from Vancouver to the Gulf Islands. They would go camping on some of the nearby islands, cooking over fires and sleeping on the beach. This was before they were teenagers.

And sometimes in the water they would hook onto the back of a moving log boom and climb onto the logs. They would wave to the crew far ahead on the tug who did not seem to mind. Could you imagine that today? Helicopters, hovercraft, police, headlines, family court, investigations, reports, televised scenarios of what could have happened in the worse case.

Then Harold said, "Once we started a little camp fire on the back of a boom and cooked our bacon on it."

That is an image so beautiful it is way beyond my imagination. A few kids cooking on a moving log boom with the Gulf Islands sliding silently by. It is terrifying. It is childhood. And in his mind they were still frying bacon while he was sitting in the coffee shop telling me about it.

They ate, waved to the crew, put out the fire, got back in their boat and chugged off with a motor just strong enough to fight the current. One image to last a lifetime, and now it is mine to last that same time.

Thanks, Harold. It's good to have old friends.

59

The Sorcerer's Sorcery

If Shakespeare was writing political news the politicians would be standing over the cauldron throwing in the promises and somehow, magically (because it makes no logical sense) pulling out the votes.

A while ago, the chief sorcerer of Canada was stirring the pot and repeating the benediction: "I love children, I love families, I love minorities. Love, love, LOVE them. And may they vote for ME." He was listed as Harper on the ballot, but his real power came when he took on the name of Sorcerer Of The Mysteries Of Voter Magic.

He also had the benediction called, "I love majorities, and little old ladies and dogs, especially puppies." But that's for another time and a different people and another spell.

Sorcerer Harper put on his magic sports jacket, not formal, not slick, but a family-friendly, backyard kind of jacket. He was having a cozy chat with a Chinese family in their freshly painted home in Richmond. It was a cozy conversation, just him and the mother and the father and the little girl surrounded by toys, a magical setting. The toys were lying on the well-trimmed lawn.

On the other side of the city-sized yard were nearly thirty

television and still cameras, some with telephoto lenses. A long lens at ten steps can get intimate moments of intimacy. A rope kept the cameras and reporters back.

The media had been bused to this typical Richmond family in their typical backyard for a photo opportunity. That was all there was to it, twenty seconds on the national news with a sorcerer in a sports jacket chatting to a typical family while the sorcerer held their child in his arm surrounded by the toys of the child. Magical.

I was not there. Reporter Marisa Thomas told me something did not look right. Marisa had just had a baby and said every mother would insist her kids pick up all their toys before company arrived.

She showed me the tape from the backyard press conference. She was right, something was wrong. The cameraman had shot all the toys and each and every one was spaced evenly from each and every other toy, almost as though some adult, such as the sorcerer's advance magicians, had taken two steps and then placed a scooter, then taken two more steps and put down a doll. Two more steps and there was a wooden puppy dog. Two more and there was a pail and shovel. Two more and there was a play bake set.

There were more toys and they were all in a radius around where the sorcerer was standing with the family. And they stopped just where the camera range would begin.

But what was really amazing was every toy was facing the same way. All the dolls were looking back at the intimate family gathering. Even the wooden dog was facing the warmth of the scene. Such a coincidence.

We drove to Richmond to speak to the family and find out how this coincidence had happened. Surely their little girl is very meticulous. But everyone was gone when we arrived; the media, the politicians, the front men, the press secretaries, the update team, the makeup woman, those who have no duties but still get paid, the security and the family, all gone now that the magic spell had been cast.

We looked over the fence. Every toy was gone. Finally the little girl had done what she should have done in the first place. It was either that or they were returned to a store by the magician's aides because they appeared unplayed with and still new.

As we were leaving, the cameraman observed that any home owner would demand his money back: "Look at that fancy paint job."

I looked, and something was not there. About as high as you could reach on the first floor of the home was a coat of new white paint. It ended just out of camera range, which was just about as high as you could reach over the sorcerer's head.

On television the house looked sparkling new. There were many paint drops on the ground as though the painting had been done in a hurry, but no one would see the paint drops because there were so many shoes standing on them. But combine the fresh paint on the walls with the toys and the toddler who was placed in the arms of the sorcerer and who was quiet for long enough to get the pictures and you had the perfect magical potion. It works every time.

What did the sorcerer say during his moments by the micro phone? I forget.

What did he promise? I forget.

What did he look like? Magically perfect.

60

The Beauty of Waiting

On the desk of Luizs is a box filled with pennies. I hope someone takes it away. It has been there for a year.

On the box is a picture of Jeneece, who was raising money for Variety, the Children's Charity.

When I first started working for Variety it was called Variety Club and they were raising money to help children with real bad problems. That was back when the telethon was held in Queen Elizabeth Theatre and all the entertainment was live. Much of it was tap dancing groups from Surrey and the audience, at least at night, was made up of street kids, some of whom were floating up near the ceiling.

But they did have a bunch of big-name performers. Variety was big even in the early 1970s. Ray Charles was performing one day and I interviewed him. We were still shooting on film then and the light needed to get an image was immense. There was a high intensity bulb on top of the camera. It could grill a steak at two feet.

"Wow, what's that?" asked Ray Charles.

"A light so we can see you," I said.

"See?" he said. "That is so passé. You see with your heart and your soul, not your eyes."

Nice.

Forty years later I still remember that, and live by that.

And forty years later Variety is still helping kids with really bad problems, like Jeneece, who is hopping over the black wires lying on the floor in the studio taking pictures. She is the size of a demitasse cup of coffee, but she is a photog, with a long lens and a desperation to get herself in the right place to take the ultimate shot of whatever it is that she is shooting.

Ten years ago Jeneece was one of Variety's special children. She has a disease that is terrible. Tumours grow throughout her body and cause massive pain. She has metal rods holding her back upright. And yet she is smiling and taking pictures. How did that happen?

Medicine and doctors, yes, massively, but something more. Determination and a self-believing gene that keeps her going. But something more. Variety helped. It gave her enough of something so that she wanted to give back. When you want to do something really important you can't be sick. You have to get to work.

She raised a million dollars for Variety with a penny drive. Can you imagine that? A million dollars with pennies? Beyond belief.

And then last year she was the official photographer for the telethon. Nice.

She took a picture of me giving money from my last book to the charity. In truth, it is not me giving the money, it is the man who founded Harbour Publishing, Howard White, who gives it.

I met Howard a long time ago when he was driving a bulldozer to support his publishing habit. He has done well. But when Variety gave an award to me for donating part of the money from these books it was really Howard. He has given more than $70,000 to Variety from the books that I have written and he has published and you have read. That is very good.

But it is nowhere near Jeneece who raised that mountain of pennies to help kids, of which she was one. That is the miracle of giving, and the miracle of wanting to give.

Eventually the penny box in the newsroom will get returned to Variety, but there is no hurry. Folks there keep putting money into it, because like Howard and Jeneece and you, there is a desire to help others.

Jeneece holding a camera to her eye and crouching in the dark to get a picture of a small child with a large problem—it's almost impossible to believe it's happening. That is more than just a story, that is more than a miracle, because that is real.

61

Grooving Through the Night

He was bouncing to thc music, which was April Wine. They were playing at the PNE. Honest to God I had never heard of April Wine, but I was working nights at the time they were famous. I missed a lot of music.

But this guy was bouncing. He was rocking. He was grooving to the sound, which was loud (so loud I left for a while and walked around the fair looking for something interesting to put on television and found the grout cleaner guy who collected rare coins to keep himself from getting bored).

He was wonderful when he was on the show the next night. He was full of life and there is nothing more you can hope for in television than to find someone who loves being alive in real life. It makes television seem real.

It was the same life I had seen in the mother and daughter on the night before at the ABBA concert. They were bopping. But the mother was a realist and she wanted a beer so she was in the beer garden.

What a stupid name. They don't grow beer there. They keep kids out of there but really, kids belong inside so that they don't see beer as a forbidden drink and find it necessary to go through a rite of passage when they grow older. If kids were allowed in beer gardens they would not suddenly OD on beer when they hit the magic age of walking past the fence.

Anyway, this woman was dancing to ABBA at the edge of the beer garden, right against the low fence that kept under-age kids out, including her teenage daughter who was on the other side of the fence also dancing to ABBA. They were sharing a pizza over the fence. They were holding hands over the fence.

But the fence was there. Thank God. It kept the teenager from being with her mother and dancing with their hips bumping to the music. Instead they bumped the fence. That would keep them pure.

And that same night with ABBA I saw another man in the crowd way far ahead of me. He was smart enough to get there early. He was bopping. He was swaying with the music. He was having a wonderful night.

He had a turban and a long grey beard.

There is hope for this country.

But back to April Wine and the guy who was bouncing and jumping and rocking. He was far in the back, so far back he could not see much of the stage. Didn't matter. He was blind.

He was bouncing his white cane into the ground. He had the beat in his blood and the music in his hand. Then he picked up his cane and like many of us do with our imaginations, he started playing the electric guitar on the slender pole of white with red tape at the end.

Watch him and he was up on the stage, even at the back of the audience.

Jump back to the ABBA concert for a moment. The teenage

girl on the outside of the fence opened her cellphone and waved it in the air. Forty years ago when her mother was a teenager the power went out at the concert at Woodstock. The singer on stage asked everyone to light a candle and wave it in the darkness.

For the next twenty years kids waved Bic lighters during concerts. Now it is the light from cellphones.

What makes a good concert? Music helps a bit. But the entertainers should pay the listeners. Without them it's just a drum without the beat.

62

Yola's Last Walk

Barb walked across the street with her violin. Her daughter, Isobel, asked, "What will you play?"

"Don't know yet. Something sad, or happy. Or both."

Caroline opened her door before they knocked.

"Thanks for coming. It will mean a lot for Alice," she said. "But Kate is taking it just as bad."

Alice is her daughter, seven years old. Kate is her neighbour and Alice's best friend, also seven. They were standing inside the house near a cardboard box.

"Anyone want a glass of wine?" Caroline asked.

A few did, and then it was time. Perry, who is Alice's father, picked up the box. Barb played something that was sad, and happy.

And they took Yola for a walk.

Kate was crying. Alice was crying. The violin was singing. Everyone, friends and neighbours, walked around their house to the backyard.

Their full names and location must remain a secret because they were breaking the law. But you know who they are; they're my neighbours. You can find them elsewhere in this book. Just don't tell the authorities about this episode.

Earlier in the day neighbour Jim had dug a hole three feet

deep in the backyard. He is newly retired and had time to do that, but he would have done it even if he had had to go to work late. Perry, with the box in his arms, had rushed home from work as early as he could.

He put the box down next to the hole behind their house.

"Can you tell us a story about Yola?" Caroline asked her daughter who was still crying.

"Yes," sob, "I remember," sob, "when she ate Beth's pizza." Then she laughed. Everyone laughed. Beth is Kate's mom and lives next door.

"And remember when she tooted in your room and we thought it was one of your fish that had jumped out of the tank and died," said Perry.

And everyone laughed again.

"And there was the time Yola pooped out the blanket," said Caroline.

More laughter. That was the locally famous story a few years ago when Yola was dying because she had not pooped for a week and the morning she was going for an expensive operation she pooped out a piece of blanket.

"Yola pooped, Yola pooped," Caroline shouted around the neighbourhood as she held up a plastic baggie that had poop and pieces of a blanket in it. Everyone cheered. Now everyone remembered, and laughed.

"I don't really like dogs," said Bruce, who is Kate's father. "I never have. But I liked Yola."

Isobel, who often walked Yola, took her mother's violin. She is what is called a teenybopper. That is often a difficult age. She had not played the violin for several years, but in that backyard she filled the darkness with beautiful music.

"It is time," said Caroline.

Perry lowered the cardboard box into the hole.

"Wait," said Alice. "Yola needs a blanket to keep her warm."

Alice and Kate spread a folded beach towel over the box.

Then they lay on the ground and reached down and put two bones and a rubber ball on top of the box. Kate tried to get one bone into the box in case she was hungry.

"Anything else?" Caroline asked.

"The picture. The picture of her babies," said Alice.

Alice and Kate ran into the house and came out with an old photo of Yola with her seven puppies born when she was a young dachshund mother. She was now eleven.

"Are you sure you want to bury that?" someone asked.

"Yes," said Alice. And she and Kate lay down again on the ground under the full moon and reached down as far as they could and placed the picture of Yola and her babies on top of the towel which was on top of the box.

"Someone has to be first," Caroline said.

And someone was. Stepping out from the group, Jim and Barb's son, Jimmy, who is full-fledged teenager, which is often a difficult age, took a shovel and spread dirt over the box.

The shovel was passed around. Beth added some dirt. Then Bruce, then Perry, and Jim and Barb and Isobel. Everyone putting dirt in and pausing, then passing the shovel on. Sarah and Leah, who are from Germany and were staying with Caroline and her family, added the final dirt. It was done.

But not so. Alice and Kate took the shovel together and together lifted a little more dirt that had been taken out of the hole and returned it to the earth, over the box.

Caroline said a two-line child's prayer.

Bruce, who doesn't believe in prayers, bowed his head.

"Now Yola is with Grandma Alice," Caroline said to her daughter, who was named after her grandmother who passed away earlier that year. Yola had been Grandma Alice's dog before it became Little Alice's. "Now Yola is back playing with Grandma," Caroline told her daughter.

Sarah had baked a banana and chocolate chip cake. Sometimes you need something sweet. Sometimes that's as good as a prayer. Everyone who wasn't on a diet took a piece, then a second. It was a good cake. Caroline said it was Barb's recipe. It's a good neighbourhood when neighbours swap recipes.

And then the doorbell in the front was ringing. Chinese food was being delivered and everyone said it was time to eat because Yola had had a really wonderful walk and would sleep quietly and peacefully, and that was just the way every night should end.

63

Platypus and the Lucky Day

I found two eggs in the refrigerator. "Today must be my lucky day," I thought because I wanted hard-boiled eggs for lunch. I put two in a pot. One egg for me, one for my wife. I told her not to make her lunch, I would give her an egg and crackers. It was twenty minutes to eight and she had to catch the eight a.m. bus and the eggs would take ten minutes.

Easy.

"Here, would you tell me if this story is any good?" she asked.

She handed me *Platypus And The Lucky Day*. This is always the best part of my morning, reviewing books that have only twelve pages and little more than a hundred words. Plus they have nice pictures.

It was platypus's lucky day, too. He found a banana in his bed and he was happy about that, and he knew today would be perfect for kite flying.

But the wind was too strong and the string broke and his kite got stuck in a tree. After that, one disaster followed another. He tried climbing the tree, but the branch broke and he fell down. He tried to paint pictures, but the rain came and made his paper soggy.

274

"This is not my lucky day," he said. So he went back to bed.

This is the kind of story that keeps you turning pages. Look, he is crying.

Then things got better. When he crawled back into bed he ate the banana he had stored under his pillow, and he also found a teddy bear he had lost under the blankets. And then he got out of bed and found a broken wagon that he fixed, and when it stopped raining he went outside and rode the wagon down a hill and crashed into a tree.

Now anyone would think things were going bad again and definitely this was not his lucky day. But suddenly the kite fell out of the tree that he'd crashed into. "It *is* my lucky day, after all," he said. It was his closing line, the most important one in the book. And the last page has a picture of platypus running with his kite flying high.

What a story. "This is great," I shouted to my wife. "It has drama. It says stick in there and don't give up. It says things will get better." It's the kind of story everyone loves.

Then I noticed I had not turned on the stove. Fifteen minutes to 8. I cranked it on high and put a cover on the pot.

"Thanks," said my wife taking the book from me. "I've got to get going, I almost missed the bus yesterday."

"What do you know about platypuses?" I asked.

"I know they are the only mammals who lay eggs, and they look like they are half duck and half beaver and they live in Australia. And now I have to go."

"You have any more books for me to read?"

"No, I have to go."

"Can you wait a minute?"

"No. Why?"

"The eggs are not quite ready."

"I don't need an egg. I have to go."

I was looking at the clock. Ten seconds, nine…etc. At zero it would be ten minutes, or maybe nine. But she was already out the door. I pulled one of the eggs out with a spoon and ran out the door after her. It is not easy to run with an egg in a spoon.

"Your lunch, wait."

She stopped and I dropped it in her book bag and tried not to look at the look she was giving me. Three minutes later she called from the bus stop.

"I missed the bus."

Me and the platypus, I was thinking. The real stories of life. I put my shoes on without socks and without tying my laces and drove around the corner, picked her up, trying again not to look at her look, and then raced after the bus.

We got to the big bus loop where she could catch it again to go to Vancouver. I stopped in the middle of traffic to let her out. I understood by some people's horns that they did not understand. I drove off as she ran across the loop.

Then she called again. "Missed it."

This is like the kite getting stuck and the branch breaking and the rain getting my picture wet all at once. I picked her up again and drove into Vancouver, without socks and without a shower and without a shave. I am not making up any of this. Life is much better than imagination.

An hour later I got home just in time to leave. I shaved in the shower, which is not a good thing to do because there was still growth on patches of my face when I got out. I put on my shoes without tying the laces and met Roger Hope at the PNE.

"This is your lucky day," he said.

He's the cameraman who is married to Deb Hope and who once bought a stack of *TV Week* magazines when his wife was on the cover and the clerk in the supermarket would not believe he was her husband. "In your dreams," is the condensed version of that story.

"There are some guys working a hundred feet up on that tower," he said excitedly to me. "This is your lucky day. Look. A high wire act right in front of us."

He was right, this was my lucky day. He began filming them and we talked to several people on the ground who expressed great admiration for anyone who would do that job.

Such a lucky day. A story of drama and excitement right off the bat. We waited, and waited, and watched. I had already written the words in my head about conquering fear and being the kings of the world. I liked it.

Then they came down. They were government safety inspectors checking the rides. "No, there's no fear and we don't want to talk."

Repeat: Government workers.

The kite just got stuck in the tree.

"Sad," said Roger.

"Don't worry. The platypus will save us."

I told him the story of the platypus.

"Are you crazy?"

"No, honest. Something good will happen."

We drove and saw a street covered with pink cherry blossoms. It was beautiful. It would be a wonderful look at a fairy land. Then a man walked down the street.

"What do you think of the blossoms?"

"Awful, rotten. Someone could slip on them. The city should clean this up, it looks messy."

The man washed away that image, just as the rain had washed away platypus's pictures.

But then we heard church bells. We did not know why they were ringing, but something must be happening. We drove to the sound, then jumped out of the truck and Roger ran down the street toward a church. The bells stopped, but he was standing under a bird house hung high in a city tree.

Who? How? We asked a woman.

"I put them there. I put bird houses everywhere."

She had thirty of them. And she had a new granddaughter. And she had built a stone wall around her yard so her granddaughter could play safely inside. And she had a pole hung with broken tea pots, which her granddaughter would love.

"What else would you do with old tea pots except make a tree out of them?" she said.

Who could not like this woman?

And she had ceramic chickens in her yard while waiting for the city to pass the law allowing real ones.

And she did not mind us taking pictures of all of the above and telling us about them.

It was a wonderful story. Just like the platypus, it was my lucky day.

The story was edited and written in one of Global's mobile satellite trucks, which was parked outside the police station on the day that the chief was telling reporters that one constable had been arrested for selling marijuana from his police car. That was not his lucky day.

"Doing the drug story?" someone who stuck his head in the open door of the truck asked.

"No, the platypus story. It has a better ending."

My wife called from the pre-school. "The kids loved the platypus story. They said they had days like that."

She also asked if I'd bought the lottery ticket she had asked for. "No. I forgot."

Jamie Forsythe, the editor who was turning the video tape into art and helping me write the last line of the story, asked what I had forgotten.

A lottery ticket, I told him. My wife says any time I dream a number I should buy a ticket with that number. I told her I had dreamed about being in a building eighty stories up. She told me to buy a ticket with eight in it. In a lifetime of using this theory it has never worked. But if it did someday it would prove that dreams can foretell the lottery.

Jamie wrote 6/49 on a piece of tape and stuck it on my phone.

Later, after we finished the story, I had some time and wanted to pass by my daughter to visit her daughters. I called ahead to make sure they were home.

She asked me if I would do her a favour.

"Of course, anything."

"It's going above and beyond," she said.

"Anything."

"No, I can't ask. It's too messy."

"Anything."

It was a thing only a trusting, loving daughter could ask. She is both. And she did.

She had a diaper that she did not want to put into her kitchen trash. When I got to the front of her building could I catch it and throw it in a dumpster around the corner? Then she would not have to bring both kids downstairs right after she had just gotten them quieted down.

"Of course."

"But don't tell anyone," she said.

"Who me, tell?" I said.

As I was putting the phone away I saw the tape, reminding me of something I had completely forgotten.

8,18,28,38,48. And because I was on my way to see three girls I added 3.

Below the open window I watched a neatly, tightly wrapped diaper in a tightly wrapped plastic bag travelling down two stories at the rapidly increasing speed of gravity hoping I would not miss. I grabbed it like a fly ball off the bat of Babe Ruth. The

279

package was break-proof, sealed and sanitary. And it was also the best catch ever, just like the last picture in the Platypus book where happy platypus is flying his kite.

I got home very happy. Life had imitated art, successfully. And in my book bag where I carry all my notes I found my uneaten egg. I did not have to boil one for the next day.

The platypus and I had the same closing line. It was a perfect day.

And 8 did not come up anywhere in the lottery, which is very good because it means I can still dream.

64

The Tale of the Tape

It was very nice that Jamie Forsythe had put tape on my phone. I left it to show my wife and anyone else who asked about it. It was a funny story.

But I am not good with electrical devices. A week later I was at my granddaughter's school for an art show. Ruby, who was then six, wanted to show me her pictures, which were on a wall near the front door.

Darn, I do not have my camera. But good news, I have my phone, which I know takes pictures, even if I am not sure how.

"Stand there and point to your picture," I said to Ruby. "This can't be hard," I said to myself as I opened my phone.

"Push the camera button," said Ruby, who, again, was six.

I saw the button and pushed it, but nothing happened. I looked at the blank screen of the phone and it was still blank.

"There's a piece of tape over the camera," said Ruby, who continued to be six while I was sixty-six and much smarter in many things.

I peeled off the tape and took her picture, which is fuzzy because it is hard to hold a phone steady and push a button at the same time. It is always good to blame your tools.

I stuck the tape back on the phone because I thought the 6/49 was such a good joke I did not want to lose it.

The next day my phone went on the fritz. The ringer was shot. I pushed a lot of buttons and got to the place where it said ring styles and loud and soft and I pushed loud, but I could not get it to ring over a whisper.

I missed a lot of calls that day. After work I went over the settings and got out the manual, but no matter what I pushed the voice of the phone was gone. Darn. I would probably have to buy a new one. Jamie had given me that phone because it was useless to him. He has three phones, all of them in the BlackBerry range. The phone he gave me was from the age of dinosaurs, almost four years old.

I was going to bring it to the phone fixit man in a phone store the next day, and got ready to spend more than I wanted to and replace it after he had told me it would cost more to fix it than to get a new one. I did not want a fancy phone, just a plain phone, but I did not know if they still sold those.

I have seen so many people who spend so much time looking at their phones, reading them and sending messages. There were two couples at a restaurant my wife and I were in. All four of the individuals had food in front of them. All four were looking at their phones. I motioned for my wife to look. She did. She shrugged. We ate. We talked. I should be chastised for not being part of the new age.

On the morning that I was going to bring my phone to the phone shop I got into a camera van with Darrell Patton.

"You know anything about phones?" I asked him.

I knew he knew everything. He was into PVRing when I was still tape recording. I showed him my phone.

"It might be that piece of tape. It's right over the ringer hole."

I did not say whoops, or anything silly. I simply took off the

6/49 tape and pushed a button. I did not explain the tape to him. I did not tell him about the camera. I just simply took off the tape like anyone would take off a piece of tape from their phone without explanation and I pushed another button and the bell was loud.

I knew that would happen. I knew that with positive thinking I could save myself a hundred dollars or more just by believing that my phone could be fixed. The only trouble is even I have trouble believing that.

65

Fiftieth Anniversary

My feet were frozen. I was standing on ice in a phone booth without a door. It was too cold to hold the phone any longer and I tried to switch it to my other hand, which was in my coat pocket, which meant I had to take it out of my pocket.

This was not easy because I had a notebook tucked under my arm.

"What'd you got?"

There was no hello. Keith Bradbury never said hello. He said "What'd you got?" He didn't ask it, he demanded it.

"I'll find something," I said.

"Well, before you do that, go down to the cop shop and find me something to lead the show with."

He didn't have time for ego stroking. He had five potentially lazy reporters at the ends of five telephones and a blank sheet of paper in front of him. By the end of the day the paper had to be filled with stories that would be turned into an hour-long show and the reporters had to supply those stories.

"And go by the court because some woman killed her husband and was being sentenced today."

He hung up. He didn't say goodbye. He had someone else to motivate with few words on the next line.

❧

No, no…that is not the way to start writing about the most meaningful half of my life. I will start again on a positive note because that half was the best of my life, outside of marriage and kids and grandkids and friends and a couple of neat vacations and some barbecued ribs that still make my mouth water. But reporting for Global in some ways was like eating ribs, with beer. It was, still is, intoxicating and sweet.

One of my granddaughters, who was then five, came into my room.

"What's that?" she asked.

"A typewriter," I said.

"What do you do with it?"

"Have the most wonderful life," I said.

She looked at the machine, which is covered with stickers and smudge marks from pencils and burns from cigarettes and more stickers and dust, and then looked at me.

"It doesn't look like fun."

I put a piece of paper in it and rolled it around and told her to hit one of the keys.

Click. Nothing happened.

"Hit it again," I said. "Harder."

She did, then again and again and she saw the skinny metal fingers coming up and letters coming out on the paper and she could spell her name, Ruby. "Wow. It's like a computer but it's not easy like a computer."

Then she typed her little sister's name, Zoe, and she kept writing. It did not matter that most of the rest of the words were a jumble of letters. It did not matter at all because that sound was the symphony of a newsroom.

Once upon a time in a world that no longer exists, the clicking of typewriters was the sound of news. Then clang, that beautiful bell at the end of each line that made Ruby look up in delight, and made me remember slamming the carriage back to start again on the next line.

"Push it like this," I said.

She did, but it didn't work.

"No, be strong. Push hard."

"But mommy says I shouldn't push things too hard."

"Sweetheart," I said while showing her, "Hard. You can't hurt it." Bang. "Your mommy grew up listening to this."

The next line the bell rang and she shoved with all her might and the music went to the old beat: type, ring, slam.

Her mother came into the room and stood still, listening. She crouched down by her daughter. "I went to sleep every night listening to that," she said to her little one.

"Your grandfather would be up typing and cursing and muttering and typing more. And then I would fall asleep. Sometimes he was still there in the morning with a lot of crumpled paper."

"A computer is easier," said Ruby.

They left to play hide-and-seek under the bed, and I was left with my old typewriter that is on a table near me, right now. The same typewriter that I got out of the garbage on my first day at BCTV. It was broken. I asked if they could get it fixed. Someone said the typewriter repairman was coming. Typewriter repairmen kept newspapers and businesses and governments alive. There is no longer such a job.

❦

"You got five minutes to finish this story. You gonna make it or do we move you down?"

That was the producer in the old BCTV newsroom. She had a cigarette in her hand and copy paper in the other and a pencil in her teeth. The newsroom had no windows and few chairs, and some of those had uneven legs.

"Be careful about falling if you type too hard," someone warned me.

The typewriters sat on a plank of wood that was held up by stacks of newspapers. That was the way a newsroom should be, handmade and rough. Besides, you were not supposed to be in the newsroom if you were reporting on news. The stories are outside.

"No, don't move me down. I'll make it. Don't worry."

Getting moved down in the lineup was like wearing a dunce cap. Besides lousing up the rhythm of the show, you looked like you couldn't do your job. And the job was simply similar to writing a school term paper in less than an hour on a subject you had never heard about three hours earlier.

In some ways that is still how news is done, except now the newsroom at Global, just as all newsrooms in the world, is quiet. Computers make no clatter, unless you turn on the button that makes it sound like a typewriter, but no one does that because the person next to you will say, "What's that?" Then you have to explain it and all you will get in response is an odd look from someone who is wondering how anyone can be as old as you.

And speaking of old, the reason for telling you all this is that Global, which was BCTV, which was CHAN, is now fifty years old, making it a child in my eyes and an ancient being in the eyes of the young reporters and editors and photographers.

There is the official history that includes many owners, and many, many presidents. It includes news being broadcast in a studio that was turned into a wrestling ring on Friday nights. But the only history I know is my time there and how I saw it through my eyes.

It came into being on Halloween evening, which was not a

great way to begin since in my observation that night has the lowest number of viewers all year:

"Let's go trick or treating."

"No, I would rather watch the news."

"Waaaaaaaa!!!"

Hence, not many viewers.

Move ahead to one of my early days at the station while sitting on a wobbly chair.

"You gonna make it?" the producer asked the reporter who was asked a few paragraphs ago. The producer stopped for a second to rub her head and take a drag on her cigarette. The newsroom was tiny and the air was filled with smoke.

"You're damn right I'll make it. I haven't missed a deadline in a month."

"A week is more like it."

"Be quiet," Brian Coxford shouted. "I'm trying to write three stories at once."

Brian was there before me, the only reporter still at the station who was there when I arrived. He looked natty in a sports jacket even at the end of the blue jeans and long-hair hippy era. And yes, he was trying to write three stories all with a deadline in one hour. Anyone who came out of those early years at BCTV learned to write fast.

That was when all news was shot on film and film was expensive and everyone was warned to take as few pictures as possible and ask as few questions as possible and still get the story.

The editing was done inside converted coat closets, each having a board on which to literally cut the film with a razor blade, (hence, you get it, cutting a story) and it was lit by a bare light bulb and all were filled with cigarette smoke.

Sometimes mistakes were made. Not often, but sometimes. A cameraman and I were doing a story on Ivy Gransom, a blind woman who participated in Polar Bear swims for more than thirty years. But on this day she was training for the Sun Run and was tearing up a track in Vancouver. She was as strong and touching as her story.

She was born blind at a time when there was no care available. Her first job as a child was cleaning out spittoons in the bars of the city. She had been married, but was not treated well. But that was all in the past. Now she was running.

The cameraman said he had an idea. He would shoot her in slow motion. He would slow her down just a little, not enough to look dumb, but you would be able to see the strength in her legs.

That sounded wonderful to me. This was at a time when there was not much you could do in the way of special effects. So before she started running he opened his film camera and turned the speed dial down.

Whoops. If you film something at a slower speed, when you play it back at normal speed it will be...oh, what will it be? Oh, no, whoops. It will be faster than normal.

At six p.m. we all gathered around a black and white television in the old basement newsroom. The story of Ivy came on. I was excited. I had only worked there a few months and I was amazed every night that something we had seen on the street was now being broadcast.

"Boy, she is running fast," someone said. "That is unbelievable. Is she really running that fast?"

I was watching Superwoman flying around the track.

"No, she is not really that fast. We screwed up," I said.

"But this is neat," someone shouted above everyone else.

"Amazing," they said.

"Unbelievably amazing," I said.

"Wow," they said.

I have never allowed slow motion or speeded-up motion or any alternative life forms to enter into a story since then unless the audience gets warned that it is happening. We can all be fooled so easily. My advice to me: Be careful and don't mess with reality. My advice to viewers and readers and listeners: Be cautious, always. It does not matter if it is the BBC or the *New York Times*. It does not matter if the reporter and editor and photographer tried with all their professional integrity to be honest, and most do. When you read or see or hear a story or facts, don't just accept them. Think about Ivy. Question what is shown to you. From government press releases to recipes, everything can be buttered up to make it look better or worse than it really is, even if it is done with good intentions.

Everyone at Global and the other TV and radio stations and newspapers tries to be accurate. It is part of the code of being a journalist and it is taken more seriously than some people's religions. If someone gets a fact wrong they will suffer not only the reprimands of management, but worse they will face their fellow reporters and editors and photographers, and those people you don't want to face.

Wrong facts mean credibility goes down the drain and then viewers and then income. So don't screw up. Get it right. The record for Global is near perfection. I am not saying that only because I love the place, I am saying that because after half my life there the number of things that have been wrong can fit inside a newborn baby's sock. Reporters and editors check and triple check. But remember Ivy, and you should do the same.

It was in the TV station that I started finding my own stories. It was that, or go through the daily pain of being assigned to the latest crime or court proceeding or political malfeasance. It came to me slowly, but it did come that documenting a shoe in the middle of the street or a couple of kids playing hopscotch was much better for my brain than the years I had spent looking at and writing about crime and depravity and corruption.

The only problem was that news runs on crime and depravity and corruption, with occasional drops of warmth and brightness.

"You've got to do crime and depravity," I was told by the boss.

"But I like little old ladies planting petunias," I said.

"Crime."

"Petunias."

"Well then, you'll do petunias where no one will see them."

Yes, that is exactly what happened. It is not a nice story, but it is true. I was put permanently behind sports at a time when not many watched sports.

"I'll show you." I said that quietly to myself because being behind sports was better than being fired. "I will try to do the best stories nobody will never see."

I wandered the streets looking for something. Anything. But the hard question was, what was I looking for?

I walked around Main and Hastings. I walked through Stanley Park and Queen Elizabeth Park and on Denman Street. That's a lot of walking and it was two p.m. and I had not found anything.

"Please," I said to no one. Okay, maybe I said it to a hole in the clouds, or the sand on the beach, or some trees. We are not going to get into religion. I believe everything is God, and I believe God doesn't much care what we believe, so long as we are nice to each other.

"Pretty please."

And on the next corner I saw a hot dog seller, from Japan. JapADogs, said his sign.

My gosh. That must be illegal. In regular storytelling years I had done stories about Hunky Bill the perogy maker who was not allowed to say "Hunky" by the people who wanted everything to be immaculately sterile and they fought him and he fought back.

He said that was what Ukrainians were called but they, the correct people, the people who know better, said "Never," and he argued—and have you ever argued with a Ukrainian? That's why the Russians gave up. Bill Konyk, better known as Hunky Bill, won. Bless him. But I had already done that story, and besides that was too much like regular news. It was a story with controversy over a name.

I kept wandering and found a shopping cart that was found in a hole in front of an apartment house in the West End. It had been buried in concrete and land fill. The apartment was getting renovated and they were digging up in front near the sidewalk and there was a shopping cart, with bottles still in it, three feet down, just like an archaeological dig. My gosh.

The building manager came out with the guy who was doing the digging and they said, "Don't know, can't imagine, I guess some guy had left it in front of the building and the next morning they poured the concrete and whoops. The cart went down the hole."

Poor old homeless bottle collector.

But bless me.

It was twenty years ago that the concrete was poured. That means that the pusher of that cart is the King Tut of Vancouver. An historic dig on Haro Street. Please, can I have a camera? Talk. Excitement. Thrills. Bingo.

You can't beat a story of instant discovery. In your life, in news, you can't. I know. I was there, instant excitement. The excitement of me calling the office afterwards.

"Hello, chief. I have a shopping cart. An old shopping cart."

"How many dead?"

"None, but the cart is fantastic. It's a Safeway cart."

"Nobody dead?"

"Maybe, but I haven't seen his bones."

"Gonna be hard to get this into the first package."

"How about the second package? The mystery of a corner of the city."

"Are you talking news, or history?"

"When you first learn history it is called news."

I didn't really say that. That would have been too intellectual. I probably said something like you won't be sorry, or some such drivel.

The story was wonderful. It made you think that sometime in the past a bottle scrounger had parked his shopping cart on this street, crawled into a bush and gone to sleep. In the late morning he got up and saw the spot where his stolen cart had been was now a concrete walkway.

Darn, he probably said, and then he left and started over again.

We were left with the image of a life that had roamed the street a generation ago. It was not big-time history, but it was real. And it had feeling. And it was real. And you could see it, so it *was* real.

"You going to put that on television?" said the chief.

"I bet they will feel for the old fellow."

The next morning, no comment on the shopping cart, only: "What'd you got today?"

Keith Bradbury was very aggressive in his assignments. Very. "Get the #@#% story and don't come back until you do."

It was assigning with an iron fist. It worked. But there is no way around saying it destroyed some people. I simply found that the impossible task of finding stories on my own day after day was much easier than the impossible task of fulfilling the assignments. Once I started I did not stop and the best part was there was little condemnation about a story that was not assigned. How could I be criticized for not doing a story as it was preconceived when it was not preconceived? Pretty smart, I thought.

But there were times assigning and finding overlapped. I was choosing the stories I liked. I loved that. And I had taken off on yet another tour of the province, this time around Cranbrook with cameraman Bill Szczur.

We drove all day to get there and found a quirky item. He filmed it, on actual film, and I interviewed. Afterwards I tried to remember what pictures he had taken and I wrote a script to go with them on a piece of scrap paper. Then came the organization of what picture came first and what comment we would use from our heroes in the story, all of this from memory.

When that was done I recorded the script on the film holding the microphone with the camera running but pointing at the sky. Any mistakes had to be done twice, or three times, but there was only ten minutes of film in a roll and we could not send in two rolls, so don't make another mistake.

And then I would go to the Greyhound Bus station and look for someone who looked kind and understanding and did not seem to hold a grudge against the world. In the 1970s this was not easy because everyone had long hair and had slogans sewn into their jean jackets saying, "Down with Everything" and the ones without slogans were protesting against something else, usually slogans.

In addition I had a bushy beard and was dressed like a back-woodsman and seldom appeared on television.

"Excuse me, but would you carry this canister of film to Vancouver and give it to a cab driver and do not open it no matter what and I'll give you five dollars?"

We had a tight budget.

What is this poor person going to carry? Drugs? Counterfeit money? Drugs? Keys to a locker with counterfeit money? Drugs?

Drugs were big in Vancouver in the '70s. Drugs are big in the '10s. There seems to be consistency there.

Okay, would YOU carry this to Vancouver? Maybe YOU?

We always found someone and all the cans got there. That is amazing.

And then Bill and I checked into a motel in Cranbrook. It was just before six p.m. and I called Keith and told him he would have a feature story for tomorrow and I knew he would be happy.

"I'm not very happy," he said. "I wanted you to call before this. I need you to go to Nelson."

"But we just checked into a hotel in Cranbrook."

"Don't tell me your troubles. I need you in Nelson, tonight."

"But."

"Forget the buts."

Keith was always fascinated by political scandal, and always there was plenty to go around. I had no interest in them and little idea of what was going on, but tonight he had found a politician in Nelson who was willing to spill the beans on someone else and we should be there to record this spilling of beans. The fact that we were in Cranbrook had nothing to do with it.

"But."

"He is waiting for you. Have the film on the midnight bus from Nelson."

Then he hung up. You cannot deal with a hung-up phone.

I told Bill and he hung down his head. You cannot deal with a hung-down head.

I went back to the desk clerk and checked out. "But we will have to charge you for..." He had to think about it. "Using the room."

"Fine."

We got our stuff out of the rooms and back into the van and started driving to Nelson. On a good day it is 220 kilometres away. But on this night it was snowing. We were up in whatever mountains separate the cities and the snow was coming down heavily. Bill was sleeping. I did not blame him. I was driving. There was not much other choice.

Somewhere between here and there with the snow coming down and headlights coming at me I pulled the wheel and whoops, we slid that way until the van stopped suddenly against something, which I could not see because it was night.

"What the **** happened?" asked Bill.

I shrugged.

This was before cellphones. Before wood or fire were discovered. We sat and watched cars passing.

"You could stop one of them," said Bill.

"How am I going to get out in the middle of a blizzard and wave down a car when they can't see me? I'll get killed."

"I'm going back to sleep," he said.

In time, a guy in a jacked-up pickup truck stopped. He was thrilled to help. He had a four-by-four, he said, and I said that was nice, whatever that was.

He hooked a chain up to our bumper and after a lot of four-wheel spinning he pulled us out. And then he left. Nice guy. He did not ask for anything or even leave his name. He had proven his four-by-four could do it.

At 10:30 we got to Nelson, found the address, Bill set up his lights, I asked the prescribed questions and got answers that I did not understand and we left, at 11:30 p.m. Just time to get to the bus station.

Asking someone at 11:35 to carry a sealed container to Vancouver when you have a beard and red eyes is different from asking someone at 5 p.m. I was almost tempted to go to $10, but I knew that inventive approach would never pass the accountant and I would be stuck for $5.

Eventually we found someone who looked like he was desperate for a handful of cash. All we had to do now was find a place to eat and sleep. This is not covered in journalism school.

Even the pizza shop was closed. There was nothing to put into our stomachs. Maybe a motel would have something. But not on this street, or that. There were no motels open, except that one.

"I don't want to go there," Bill said.

"Me neither."

But we went because it was the only one. With nothing to eat I looked at my room. One bare light bulb, one large water pipe over the bed, one worn bed underneath it. I kept on my boots, and my toque, and pulled it down over my face, and put on my raincoat, which was plasticized polyester, and wrapped it around myself and lay down on the bed, and slept.

In the morning we got bacon and eggs and drove back to Cranbrook.

The only thing Keith said on the phone was, "What'd you got for today?"

On the other hand, Keith's son-in-law, Oliver Lum, who is now the assistant assignment editor, saw only a kind and gentle man at home. I know that Keith was a good and patient husband and father who never raised his voice. But in the newsroom he was the archetype of the old-fashioned hard-nosed editor who sent terror through the phone lines. Maybe he thought it could not be done any other way.

Clive Jackson, who was a super reporter, became Bradbury's intermediary between himself and the reporters. This was during a time when Bradbury would not speak to his reporters and they would not speak to him. Yes, it was a very rough place to work. Clive suffered more than everyone else. He was like the first sergeant working under a fire-breathing captain. He could not win.

Twenty years later Clive has taken over being totally in charge of all the stories that are assigned, except he does it with wit and guile and by complimenting and encouraging and sometimes downright fibbing to a reporter: "You are the only one who can do this."

He swears he means it when he says that. And everyone says, "Did he use that line on you again?" But it works. Compliments, even ones you don't believe when you hear them, you pretend are true.

The result is he gets the same work done, often better work than in the past, without causing pain. That alone is a story that should be taught in all management schools.

Cameron Bell was the news director during this tumultuous time when Bradbury was the assignment editor. He is truly a legend in television news. He was really the philosopher king who created the BCTV style of having the pictures tell the story. He gave more credit and responsibility to photographers and editors than to reporters. He once ordered reporters to be banned from the edit rooms until the editor had created the story.

"What do you mean I can't go in there? It's my story." Thus sayeth the reporter.

"It is not your story. It is OUR story." Thus sayeth the news director, meaning the assigning, the shooting, the editing and the reporting were the story.

And when the reporter was allowed to enter the dark edit room he or she was told: "You will write to the picture, understand? The pictures are more important than you. You will say very little and you will say it well and then you will shut up." All television newsrooms should have that engraved in their ceilings so that when reporters lean back in their chairs in deep reporter-like thought they will see all they need to know.

But Cameron did not fit the corporate image. He had a big, bushy beard and often put his feet up on the desk, even when he was in someone else's office. He was a genius at the grassroots level. For years he worked under Ray Peters, whom I never got to know. Mr. Peters owned BCTV and believed in news and gave Cameron a free hand to do whatever he had to do to make the ratings go up. Mr. Peters was worshiped by his employees, and that is a good thing because when you are a good boss you have good employees.

During this era in the late 1970s and early 1980s the ratings sky-rocketed. From a baby television station it became a giant almost overnight. I was in the basement newsroom in 1977 when the ratings agency said we had half a million viewers. In a province that had only two-and-a-half million people, that was phenomenal. That was a higher percentage than any national US news show.

Whatever was working, it was working.

But after Mr. Peters left, Cameron did not fit in with the new owners and management. He still had his feet on the desk. A genius, yes, but there were those feet.

Carpet city fired him. One of the many new regimes of power that came in upstairs, where there was actual carpet on the floor instead of old scripts lying around, did not like his down-home style.

The only lesson here is that life is not fair.

One good thing: the man who fired him was later fired by the next owners. Of course, that does not help you if you have been fired.

But in the first quarter century that I worked at BCTV it was Cameron Bell and Keith Bradbury who created the hard-driving, picture-oriented storytelling that pushed the station to number one.

I was also in the old, underground newsroom with a small crowd of editors and reporters, mostly sitting on stacks of newspapers and watching the show on a ten-inch black-and-white TV with rabbit ears when it was announced that we had passed CBC, which had been number one.

We did not even have coffee to cheer with.

Soon after that we moved into the new newsroom with desks and, most of all, windows. But it was quickly discovered that, since the idea was to broadcast the show from the newsroom, the windows let in too much sunlight, which is the wrong kind of light for the cameras and everything looked blue. So drapes were installed. So much for looking out. But the room did have typewriters, so not only was it still a newsroom, it still sounded like one.

The news director now, Ian Hayson, was a reporter at the *Province* when I was a reporter at the *Sun*. The lesson there is some people are smarter than me. Ian also has a beard, and he does put his feet on the desk. That is a good sign.

Ian did teach me one profound thing, and it had nothing to do with news. He knew he was going to deepen my perception of everything with one short story.

He said he had met an old friend whom he had not seen in a while. "My friend told me he was going to visit his sister who had diabetes," said Ian.

"I told him what a coincidence, I just found out I have diabetes, too. Now I have to watch my diet."

Then Ian told me that his friend said, "Probably not like my sister. She's had her two legs and one arm amputated. And now she is going blind."

I don't know how to express it, and Ian did not either, but in that short exchange is everything you need to know about the realities of putting things, like your own problems, into perspective. It is one of those eternal lessons good for carrying around in an easily accessible part of your head. It is a story that changes a life.

If you want to go far in news, or business, or politics, or life, think of Ian's story.

With Ian and Clive guiding the news and a room full of people typing quietly on computers, the news that is now on the air is incredibly good. Those who say the old days were better are romantically involved with a truth that exists more in their imagination than their memory. In the old days they said the old days were better. According to one brilliant song title: *These Are The Good Old Days.*

How does it work?

The cameramen are the infantry. There is not a bad one out there. They stand in the rain and snow, and their fingers are frozen and they still try to outdo themselves every day.

The editors are crazy. I have said this publicly since my first day in television. They spend their lives in little rooms with no windows looking at small screens and trying to put pictures together in a way that makes sense in a story that seldom goes longer than two minutes. This would drive anyone crazy. And, like the photographers, they get no credit for their work.

And though I work one step away from intimacy with the picture takers and the picture cutters, I basically never see another reporter. Reporters are out in the field half the day and in edit rooms the other half. A deep conversation with another reporter is "Hello" or "Good night." Seldom are both said to the same person on the same day.

One of the few I know a bit is John Daly, who is as crazy as an editor but he gets to see the sunlight. He lives by scoops, like an old-fashioned newspaper reporter, which he used to be. Some of the older cameramen say he is like a cat with his claws hooked into the inside roof of the camera van, hanging there and shouting, "Go, go, go!" How he got the Glen Clark story of the police raiding the premier's house is still a mystery. Whether you agree with that kind of news or not is irrelevant. He got the story, and that means he is an incredible reporter.

I've heard he seldom sleeps. He is on the phone through the night with his contacts. Yes, crazy. But amazing.

And there is Brian Coxford, the longest surviving reporter at the station. He is simply the best all-round reporter in British Columbia, maybe Canada. You can give him any subject at nine a.m. to cover and by six p.m. he has the top story in the province. The only problem is it is always five p.m. when he gets back to edit, unless it is five-thirty.

"Where is he?"

Every day you hear that. Most stories take at least two hours to put together.

"He can't possibly make it on time."

But he does, every day. He is also the best-dressed reporter. In truth, he dresses better than the anchors who get large clothing allowances.

I once asked Brian what was the hardest part of going on urgent out-of-town trips. I thought he would say research or lining up contacts.

"Picking what I'll wear," he said.

"What'd you mean? I just put on my coat and shoes," I said.

"But which coat and which shoes," he said.

"But you are going into the bush."

"So? That has its own style. You can't look too good, or too bad."

He is good, and sharp.

There is also Darlene Heiderman, who is one of the toughest-tenderest women I know. She seems to cover all the murders that John Daly can't squeeze into his schedule.

I don't say hello to her. I say, "Who got killed today?"

Before she became a reporter she was a cook in a forestry camp. She kept a loaded shotgun near the stove.

What I admired most about her was that during the awful,

gut-wrenching Robert Pickton investigation and trial she was the main reporter. She also had a new baby. She would bring her infant son to work and he would play on a blanket by her feet while she would be writing stories of the most horrific and brutal murders on the pig farm.

Some day her kids will say to her, like all kids do, "Mom, you don't understand how hard our lives are."

And she will probably say to them, "You are right, sweetheart. Tell me your troubles. I have never known pain like you have."

And there is Linda Alyesworth, who never tires of doing stories about the plight of frogs or whales. She is called The Teacher by the cameramen and editors because all her stories make you think you are in school and you are now going to learn something important, so sit up and pay attention. She never loses her enthusiasm.

But what is most amazing about Linda is she did not come from a journalism school like most others. She did it the old-fashioned way. She worked her way up. She started as a production assistant with a stopwatch counting down the seconds left in each story as it was on the air. It is step one. She climbed all the way to the top, so when others say to her, "How can I be a reporter? What's the secret, what's the trick? Do I need a new hairdo?" she says simply, "Start somewhere, and don't stop."

And behind the scenes there's Karl Avefjall. He is an editor, but he is more than that; he is a legend. He is fascinated by war and armies and knows the outcome of every battle in every war ever fought. No, I am not exaggerating.

He grew up wearing an apron and cleaning off tables in his mother's coffee shop in the basement of the old police station on Main Street. One day he asked a reporter if he could visit the television station. One look inside and he decided he wanted to be an editor.

He did not go to school or have any training. He just watched and learned and hung around and almost thirty years later he is still there basically producing and writing and editing one story after another, with no credit or applause or recognition. But don't get your facts wrong about a war. You will lose.

The lesson: You see something you want to do, and you do it. No whining, no complaining that it can't be done or you can't do it or you have to go to school and the school has a long waiting list and so you can't be expected to do that, or anything. Do what Karl did. You want it, do it. You can win a war or get a job.

Luca Sgaetti did the same. He is another brilliant editor whom you never see. He just followed his father to work one day and also said he would like to learn to edit. There was no school or diploma. He watched and learned and is now one of the people who make stories shine. He is close to being a genius but like so many others he gets no recognition. The show is carried by an army of people who do the impossible day after day, but you never see or hear about them.

And there is Ted Chernecki, an amazing reporter but also a computer nutcase. He sits elbow to iPad with me and for years we have struggled to find something in common to say to each other.

I think he is wonderful. He was an anchor who stepped down and went back to reporting. He gave up the fame and got back to the street asking questions and trying to figure out what the heck is going on. It was more exciting than being in the office all day, he said. I agree.

But he loves computers and has them at his fingertips and on his lap and in his pockets. He keeps trying to show me what is new. He is always excited about them. I keep trying to understand, but get lost on the first app.

On my desk are little plants that Karen Deeney, the chief

editor, brings in. The plants are dying and we try to bring them back to life with water and care. Some of them go under my desk at night to get darkness. This is not a computer-friendly area.

But Ted wants to show me his latest cellphone, which can take a picture of me sitting in front of my office-issued computer, beam the image up to a satellite and send it back to my computer. Me, sitting there looking stupid tending my desk-sized garden, is now on my computer in live action.

"This is the future of news," said Ted. "Wherever you are, you can put it on live. You can see it as it is happening."

He is right. He is way ahead of me.

But on the other hand, when I started in newspapers in the early 1960s we had the same kind of excitement. I would be at the murder scene of a gangland mobster in Lower Manhattan. I was just a cub reporter but working with the old pros. The body is on the street. The reporter sees what he sees, talks to the cops, takes out a dime and calls the city desk.

"Big time murder," the reporter says.

He was then transferred to a rewrite man. They were always men, even if they were women. The writers were brilliant. Many of them had a string of novels behind their names.

"Mobster shot ten times outside oyster bar," said the reporter.

Rewrite man asked questions. There were rubber bands holding up his shirt sleeves and a cigar was between his teeth, even if he was a she. Words were pounded together at incredible speed, words that would send a chill through readers on the subway riding under the bloody street.

The type-written pages went down to the composing room, a vast area of printer's hell where open gas-fed flames melted zinc ingots that dripped into linotype machines where operators made every line the same length. Then the hot type, which cooled in the smoky night air, was pounded into a steel form and sent to the presses, which were stopped for big news events. Yes, someone actually said, "Stop the presses."

And a few minutes later the papers came out at the end of the conveyor belt with the headline MOBSTER KILLED AT OYS-TER BAR.

The newspapers were loaded onto trucks and driven back to the crime scene and dropped off where the cops would pick them up and read about the crime while standing over the body that was still on the street. That was instant news.

No satellites needed. But Ted is right. News is headed for a revolution as big as the Gutenberg press. I wish I was starting all over again.

And there is Jas Johal who grew up in Williams Lake with a father who worked in a sawmill. Today he is Global's correspondent in India. Wow! How?

"I really wanted it. I grew up watching BCTV and wanted to do that," he said.

That's the answer for everything. So simple. So true. Follow what Jas said and you can do anything you want to do.

Follow what Ted does and you can shock the world, again.

There are so many other good reporters and editors and cameramen. In fact there are no bad ones. Some of them are crazy, but with passion for their jobs. If I wasn't working there I would still watch the show. Randy McHale, who looks like he is nine feet tall but seldom stands up, has spent a lifetime organizing the stories so that chaos makes sense. He is the producer of the *News Hour* and when one story goes into another and you say, "Oh, yeah, I get it now," it is because of him.

And Tim Perry, another guy whom you never see, writes magic for stories that lift them from hard-to-understand to "Wow, did you hear that?" You have never seen his face or his name. He is like so many behind the scenes making it OUR story.

And there is the new chief number one anchor, Chris Gailus. He came in like a deep breath of fresh air. He is a chief anchor who shows up for work in the morning, goes to story meetings, writes his own scripts, reads all of the copy before he goes on the air and actually goes out and reports on stories that take him out of the office.

That was all a big shock, and it is good that he is here. Ratings have also gone up. I told him he made me wish I was starting over in my career.

At home my typewriter still sits near me, waiting. My granddaughter will come visiting again soon and start typing on it. I will stop whatever I am doing and just listen. We will both be in the same room, but I will be in another world.

66

Back to the Picture Books: A Nursery Story

You have to end on an up note, always, no matter what you are talking about.

Come to think of it, there are no other notes here. Even the deaths have their beauty.

But this was amazing.

It was like most days and most lives. We were looking for a story, as always, and looking, and it was late.

We stopped at Main and 27th Avenue because there was a bicycle chained to a pole. There is always a reason to stop and look at something.

The bike had artificial flowers wrapped around its handlebars and seat. Nice, but no one was around except a woman pushing a baby carriage, and it was getting later.

"We will find something good on this block," I said. "We will and we will be done in twenty minutes."

How do you make a prediction like that and stay sane? You

cannot predict the future. It is impossible. You can only predict how you will approach the future, but you can't change it.

Wrong.

By myself, the cameraman staying behind with his van, which was illegally parked, I walked up the street. To cut it short, there was a junk shop near the end of the street that we had found love in a year earlier, although I had forgotten about that.

Jim, who owned the shop, and Kristie were holding hands while sitting on the sidewalk in old, junk chairs that were for sale, cheap. That was last year. They had met in a junk shop, which was romantic. Their love was new, which was romantic. He said they were in love. In fact, Jim shouted that they were "in LO-O-O-OVE," which of course was totally romantic. And they were beaming and glowing, like they had just discovered something wonderful, which is what love does.

We put them on television because it was sweet and they were in front of a junk shop.

I walked into the shop a year later.

"What's new?"

"Nothing much," said Jim. "We had a baby and I've sold the shop to have more time with the baby."

Darn, I thought. I had only heard that he sold the shop. The door behind me was open and the traffic of Main Street had drowned out the rest of his words. How much do we all miss because a truck goes by when the punchline is delivered?

"Recession?"

"No, baby."

"Baby? You and Kristie had a baby?"

How many sales did he lose because the door had been open?

"Yes, baby."

"Where? When? Can we see him-her?"

"She's a her, and you just missed her. Kristie is on her way home. She and the baby are heading toward 12th and Main. She might be going for a coffee. She's wearing green."

By this time Dave the cameraman had joined me and heard we were going to be chasing someone going north. He had just walked south after finding a legal parking spot two blocks away. Such is life.

We ran back to his van. He drove around the block and we passed the bike with the flowers but the traffic was heavy on Main and it was hard to get out onto the street.

"Now, go now."

"No. We'll be killed."

"But we've got to find her before she goes for coffee or something."

Despite the urgency in my voice, Dave was smart. He waited until "now" had an opening big enough to get his truck into.

And then we headed north. He was looking and I was looking and by now she could be in any one of the twenty-one coffee shops between 12th and 27th. Yes, there are that many. I did a story on all of them, and all of them are making money, which proves you should have invested in coffee instead of the stock market.

And right at this moment Kristie might be in one of them giving them more money and we will not find her, and it was getting later.

"There," said Dave or me. "There, that's the same woman who passed us when we were looking at the bike." How tiny is the world?

He made an illegal U-turn and parked illegally in a no-stopping zone and we jumped out and she stopped.

I said, "Hi."

Can you picture how absurd this is? A woman is pushing a baby carriage and two guys jump out of an SUV basically right in front of her and one says, "Hi."

"Hi," she said.

There is a self-assured woman. Then she recognized me.

"I heard that you and Jim, you know," I said pointing at the baby.

"Yes, this is Lucy."

What more can you possibly want in life? When I left Jim and Kristie they were sitting in used chairs with price tags on them holding hands and looking into each other's eyes. And now out of the two there were three. That is math that is not possible in math classes, and that is why it is a miracle.

"I'll tell you a secret," said Kristie. "On the day you talked to us last year I had just heard the baby's heart beat."

"But you didn't tell us," I said.

"No."

Of course not. We were a wandering news crew. You don't tell secrets to people who tell everything to the world. In fact, you don't tell secrets to anyone if they are precious and you want them to remain a secret.

"We were so happy that day," Kristie said.

Later I looked at the tape from that day, almost exactly one year earlier to the day. Jim had said they were "in LO-O-O-OVE." Kristie had been glowing. That is more than just plain everyday love. That is LO-O-O-OVE with three being made out of two, which is impossible on a blackboard or a calculator.

Kristie walked back to the junk shop and Jim took his daughter and sat in an old junk chair in front of the shop that was no longer his so that he would have more time with his daughter. He would work just a few days a week. Kristie sat next to him in a junk shop chair and they looked like they did a year ago, except one thing was new.

It is the oldest story of the human race, that we tell over and over again with unbelievable excitement because not only is it a miracle and impossible to get three from one plus one, but it is always new.

Tell the folks around the dinner table that someone had a new baby and you won't have to say another word. You will make the night for them. Guaranteed.

THE END

But it is not. I have an assignment for you, and you know what it is. Find a story, bring it home and you will make the night better for everyone, including yourself. You will not need that positive thinking stuff. Your life will be positive.

Rule Number One: Guaranteed.